MAKING YOUR MIND MATTER

Strategies for Increasing Practical Intelligence

Vincent Ryan Ruggiero

ROWMAN & LITTLEFIELD PUBLISHERS, INC.

Lanham • Boulder • New York • Oxford

ROWMAN & LITTLEFIELD PUBLISHERS, INC.

Published in the United States of America
by Rowman & Littlefield Publishers, Inc.
A Member of the Rowman & Littlefield Publishing Group
4501 Forbes Boulevard, Suite 200, Lanham, Maryland 20706
www.rowmanlittlefield.com

PO Box 317
Oxford
OX2 9RU, UK

British Library Cataloguing in Publication Information Available

Library of Congress Cataloging-in-Publication Data

Ruggiero, Vincent Ryan.
  Making your mind matter : strategies for increasing practical
intelligence / Vincent Ryan Ruggiero.
    p. cm.
  Includes bibliographical references and index.
ISBN 0-7425-1462-5 (hardcover : alk. paper)—ISBN 0-7425-1463-3
    (pbk. : alk. paper)
1. Intellect. I. Title.
BF431.R78 2003
153.9—dc21

                                                              2003008107

Printed in the United States of America

∞™ The paper used in this publication meets the minimum requirements of
American National Standard for Information Sciences—Permanence of Paper
for Printed Library Materials, ANSI/NISO Z39.48-1992.

To my wife Barbara
for her support, encouragement,
understanding, and, most of all,
for her patience

and

To the memory of my father
who was fond of saying that the
head was meant to be more than
a hat rack

CONTENTS

4 Testing Ideas   49

*Ideas are to the mind as food is to the body. And the
rule governing their consumption is the same: Examine
carefully before swallowing.*

5 Recognizing Errors in Reasoning   59

*An important characteristic of a quality mind is the
ability to detect flaws in other people's reasoning and to
purge them from one's own.*

   We might as well give up the fiction
   That we can argue any view.
   For what in me is pure Conviction
   Is simple Prejudice in you.
   —Phyllis McGinley

   Morality, like art, consists in drawing the line somewhere.
   —Gilbert Keith Chesterton

> *To do all the talking and not be willing to listen*
> *is a form of greed.*
>   —Democritus of Abdera

INTRODUCTION

The Neglect of the Mind[a]

American education has neglected students' minds for a century and everyone has been affected. Knowing how this tragedy happened is the first step toward reversing its effects in your life.

If you are like most people, your educational experience consisted essentially of being given information to remember. The formula for academic success was to read the textbook carefully, listen attentively to teachers' lectures, and regurgitate the data on examinations, which generally required you to mark "T" or "F," choose among items "a" through "d," or fill in some blanks. On the rare occasions when an essay question was included, it typically called for you to repeat what the textbook author or your teacher said, preferably verbatim.

If this has been your experience, you may be surprised to learn that it didn't have to be that way. Teachers could have treated your mind as a factory for producing and refining ideas of your own rather than as a warehouse for other people's ideas. The emphasis would have been not only on *possessing* information but, more importantly, on *using* it to solve problems and resolve issues. The benefit to you would have been greater intellectual independence and competence in and out of the classroom.

---

[a] The material in this introduction was copyrighted in 2003 by MindPower, Inc. and is used with permission.

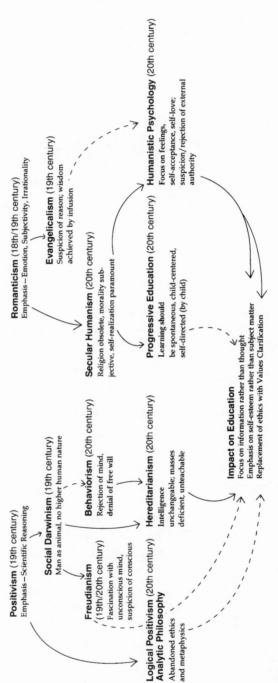

The Enlightenment Legacy
[Solid line indicates direct connection; broken line, indirect]

Positivism (19th century)
Emphasis — Scientific Reasoning

Social Darwinism (19th century)
Man as animal, no higher human nature

Freudianism (19th/20th century)
Fascination with unconscious mind, suspicion of conscious

Behaviorism (20th century)
Rejection of mind, denial of free will

Hereditarianism (20th century)
Intelligence unchangeable; masses deficient, unteachable

Logical Positivism/ Analytic Philosophy (20th century)
Abandoned ethics and metaphysics

Romanticism (18th/19th century)
Emphasis — Emotion, Subjectivity, Irrationality

Evangelicalism (19th century)
Suspicion of reason; wisdom achieved by infusion

Secular Humanism (20th century)
Religion obsolete, morality subjective, self-realization paramount

Humanistic Psychology (20th century)
Focus on feelings, self-acceptance, self-love; suspicion/rejection of external authority

Progressive Education (20th century)
Learning should be spontaneous, child-centered, self-directed (by child)

Impact on Education
Focus on information rather than thought
Emphasis on self-esteem rather than subject matter
Replacement of ethics with Values Clarification

Figure I

Why were you denied that superior kind of education? The answer lies in a dispute that began approximately three hundred years ago.

The historical period known both as the Enlightenment and the Age of Reason occurred during the late seventeenth and early eighteenth centuries. The reigning idea of that period was that reason is the only trustworthy source of knowledge. This idea produced two powerful reactions, one supportive and the other opposing. The supportive reaction, *Positivism*, emphasized scientific investigation, objectivity, and logic; the opposing one, *Romanticism*, emphasized imagination, subjectivity, and emotion. Every major intellectual movement in the nineteenth and twentieth centuries can be traced, at least in part, to one of these reactions. Education, in particular, has been profoundly affected by them.[b] (See figure 1.) We will examine the influence of Positivism first, then that of Romanticism.

THE INFLUENCE OF POSITIVISM

Positivism's emphasis on scientific reasoning not only brought greater prominence to biology, chemistry, and physics, it also contributed to the marginalization of philosophy. Before the Enlightenment, philosophy was a broad discipline with four main divisions—ethics, metaphysics, epistemology, and logic—and its aim was the pursuit of wisdom. (The word *philosophy* derives from a Greek word meaning "love of wisdom.") Eventually, however, Logical Positivism and Analytic Philosophy abandoned ethics and metaphysics and surrendered epistemology to cognitive psychology. As a result, philosophy was reduced to formal logic and linguistic analysis and was denied a role in the development of modern education.

Positivism also led to Social Darwinism, the extension of Darwin's theory of natural selection to human behavior. In regarding man as merely an animal, Social Darwinists rejected the idea of a higher human nature. This viewpoint was adopted, as well, by three psychological movements that either denied or

---

[b] The Enlightenment did not, of course, invent itself. It was the product of a number of historical forces, chief of which was the tension between faith and reason. This tension can be traced to early Christianity. Though Jesus's use of metaphor, analogy, and most notably parable invited and in many cases *required* his followers to use reason, the preaching emphases of the Apostles, notably Paul, led some to believe that faith and reason were opposed. In the Middle Ages, Thomas Aquinas argued for the compatibility of faith and reason, but Martin Luther's denial of free will and famous formula, "only faith, only grace, only Scripture," disparaged reason (and free will) and helped to pave the way for the Enlightenment reaction.

disparaged the thinking mind: Freudianism held that conscious mental activity only served to disguise the unconscious; Behaviorism rejected the human mind and free will altogether; Hereditarianism posited that human intelligence is unalterable.[c]

The influence of Hereditarianism was especially strong in education. In the first two decades of the twentieth century, a group of American scholars asserted that intelligence is inherited, most people possess but a small portion of it, and nothing can be done to repair their deficiency. During World War I, the scholars sought to prove this idea scientifically by administering an IQ test to 1.75 million army recruits. The test, now known to have been seriously flawed in design and administration, was then hailed as the definitive study of human intelligence.[d] It "proved" that the average mental age of northern European adults was about thirteen years; of southern and central European adults, about eleven and a half years; and of Black adults, about ten years.[1]

This test provided a "scientific" basis for diluting education, and Hereditarian writings further advanced the cause. Henry Goddard wrote, "There are great groups of men, laborers, who are but little above the child, who must be told what to do and shown how to do it; and who, if we would avoid disaster, must not be put into positions where they will have to act upon their own initiative or their own judgment."[2] Edward Thorndike argued that because of these limitations, education should focus on gratifying students' impulses rather than developing their minds.[3]

Moreover, some philanthropic groups put their influence and money at the service of the Hereditarian program. For example, Frederick Taylor Gates, a Rockefeller financial advisor, announced

> We shall not try to make these people or any of their children into philosophers or men of learning, or men of science. We have not to raise up from among them authors, editors, poets or men of letters. We shall not search for embryo great artists, painters, musicians nor lawyers, doctors, preachers, politicians, statesmen, of whom we have an ample supply. The task we set before ourselves is very simple as well as a very beautiful one, to train these people just as we find them to a perfectly ideal life just where they are.[4]

---

[c] The great irony of Positivism is that all the movements it produced spurned its central focus, reason.

[d] It should be noted that the IQ test was developed for the sole purpose of identifying students with learning difficulties and that its originator, Alfred Binet, warned against using it to test overall intelligence.

These and similar efforts resulted in a number of changes in American education. Vocational training displaced traditional academic education: between 1900 and 1940, the percentage of courses devoted to the development of students' minds declined from 75 percent to 20 percent.[5] In addition, the organizational structure of the school was revised to match that of the factory. Principals became managers; teachers became workers who made few (if any) decisions themselves but, instead, slavishly followed the prescribed program. (Incidentally, both the American Federation of Labor and the National Association of Manufacturers supported this arrangement.)

Not surprisingly, teachers were trained to tell students *what* to think rather than teach them *how* to think. Textbooks were filled with information to be remembered rather than exercises in analysis and judgment. And tests measured recall of minutiae rather than understanding and application of concepts and principles. Moreover, to minimize the risks of noncompliance, women were chosen over men for teaching posts and paid relatively little. In 1870, half of all teachers had been women; by 1920, 86 percent were.[6]

As one commentator noted, the effect of these changes was to build mental calculators instead of minds. In this system, he observed, "Fact is added to fact, until the sum of the facts is equal to graduation."[7]

THE INFLUENCE OF ROMANTICISM

Jean-Jacques Rousseau has been called the "Father of Romanticism." Rousseau rejected the Enlightenment view of reason and intellect and declared that "the state of reflection is contrary to nature, and . . . the man who meditates is a depraved animal." Believing that emotion is a more reliable guide to living than thought, he declared, "All that I *feel* to be right, is right; whatever I *feel* to be wrong is wrong" (emphasis added.) Rousseau also challenged the classical idea that good tendencies and evil tendencies struggle for dominance within each person. In his view, everyone is born good, whatever impulses and desires spring forth from that "natural" self are necessarily wholesome, and corruption comes only from the process of socialization. (He once called reading "the curse of childhood.") This perspective also found expression in Rousseau's personal life. After abandoning each of his children at birth, he rejected responsibility for his actions and blamed instead the "wealthy class." In keeping with his theory about the nature of humanity, Rousseau idealized those who are least influenced by society and, in his view, still possess their natural innocence—the child, the peasant, and the "Noble Savage."[8]

Rousseau's Romanticism has remained influential from his own eighteenth century to the present time. Paradoxically, his ideas have found expression both in Christianity and in Christianity's most prominent rival, Secular Humanism.

The Evangelical movement was the largest and most influential religious movement in America to embrace Romanticism's disdain for reason.[e] In 1853, Bela Bates Edwards, a Protestant clergyman, described the prevailing attitude in his "impression, somewhat general, that an intellectual clergyman is [considered] deficient in piety, and that an eminently pious minister is [considered] deficient in intellect."[9] This attitude prevailed long after Edwards categorized it. As recently as 1994, Evangelical scholar Mark Knoll observed that "the scandal of the evangelical mind is that there is not much of an evangelical mind."[10] Another contemporary Evangelical scholar, Os Guinness, has lamented the fact that "most evangelicals simply don't think."[11] Unfortunately, Evangelicals' opposition to reason prevented them from recognizing emotion as an equal, if not greater, threat to religion, as well as to education.

Secular Humanism was also Rousseauvian in spirit, rejecting traditional religion and all absolutes, including moral ones, and affirming personal autonomy and free will. However, Secular Humanism also had a Positivist dimension. The tension between the two dimensions was most evident in the Progressive Education movement founded by a leading Secular Humanist, John Dewey. Dewey's philosophy was a blend of two opposing ideas. On the one hand, he regarded the training of the intellect as essential to education.[12] On the other, he followed his Rousseauvian mentor Francis Wayland Parker ("the spontaneous tendencies of the child are the records of inborn divinity"[13]) and defined education as a process of *growth* rather than *socialization*. Dewey's followers rejected Dewey's commitment to the mind and made Progressive Education permissive, indulgent, and mindless.[14]

By far the most significant cultural force from 1950 to the present has been Humanistic Psychology. This psychological movement has shaped the contemporary view of self, relationships, and the meaning of life. It has also contributed goals and methods for schools, corporations, and advertising agencies, and provided a guiding philosophy for modern entertainment. The success of Humanistic Psychology lay in its connection both to Secular Humanism and liberal, "modernist" Christianity. Though the former was

---

[e] It is often said that the Puritans were anti-intellectual, but as Richard Hofstadter and others have documented, they placed great value on learning, establishing numerous libraries, Harvard College, and a system of lower schools, and emphasized not only religious studies but also the pagan classics as well.

technically atheistic and the latter technically theistic, the human person (rather than God) was central to each. As Richard Hofstadter notes, when "modernist" Protestantism eliminated Christian doctrine, nothing remained but "the subjective experience of the individual."[15]

The names most closely associated with Humanistic Psychology are Carl Rogers and Abraham Maslow. Both men were influenced by John Dewey's thought while at Teachers College, Columbia University, Rogers as a student and Maslow as an instructor. Both were later, on separate occasions, chosen "Humanist of the Year." In addition, both were influenced by the ideas of the "modernist" Christian ministers, Harry Emerson Fosdick and Norman Vincent Peale. Fosdick wrote about self-development in 1932 and about discovering, accepting, and loving oneself in his 1943 book, *On Being a Real Person*. Peale wrote about self-realization in 1932 and again in 1952 in his famous book, *The Power of Positive Thinking*. Considerably later, Maslow set forth his idea of self-actualization (1954) and Rogers wrote *On Becoming a Person* (1961).[16]

The connection between Rogers and Rousseau is nowhere more evident than in this passage from Rogers: "One of the basic things which I was a long time in realizing, and which I am still learning, is that when an activity *feels* as though it is valuable or worth doing, it *is* worth doing. Put another way, I have learned that my total organismic sensing of a situation is more trustworthy than my intellect" (Rogers's emphasis). Rogers also held that "the basic nature of the human being . . . is constructive and trustworthy," "experience" is the only authority, nothing in life is fixed, and feelings are "a competent and trustworthy guide to behavior." His prescription for therapy was never to direct the client and never to judge. For the classroom, he recommended giving no grades but letting students evaluate their own progress.[17]

In *A Way of Being*, Rogers wrote, "I would like to treasure the ideas that emerge. . . . I like the behavioral impulses—appropriate, crazy, achievement-oriented, sexual, murderous. I want to accept all of these feelings, ideas, and impulses as an enriching part of me. I don't expect to act on all of them, but when I accept them all, I can be more real."[18] And in a chapter titled "Do We Need a Reality?" he denied the idea of objective reality independent of the person observing it. Instead, he argued that each person has his or her own reality, which may change from day to day.

Abraham Maslow shared many of Rogers' ideas but was more reflective than Rogers and thus, over the years, revised some of his views. For example, in the second edition of *Motivation and Personality*, published sixteen years after the first edition, he acknowledged that he had failed to realize that gratification of every desire could become a "pathology."[19] And his journals, published in 1979, revealed that he had become troubled by other emphases in the Humanistic Psychology he had helped to found.

For example, in his journal, Maslow expressed concern over the idea that the child is by nature good and admitted that he had not clarified that self-esteem depends on achievement. He also wrote to himself: "One trouble with liberals, humanists . . . Esalen, Rogers, [and others] is in their giving up of evil, or at least their total confusion about it," and "they can't get really indignant at a wrong (unless it's fashionable to, [and] the whole pack does) because they don't really know right from wrong." One causative factor, he said, was "Rousseauistic Utopianism" and he noted that Rogers was guilty of it.[20] Maslow's willingness to correct his errors was laudable. Unfortunately, once the basic formulas of Humanistic Psychology were promulgated and popularized, they proved difficult, if not impossible, to change.

We have noted that Hereditarianism diluted education, removing rigor and substituting the transfer of information for the training of students' minds. For all its faults, however, the mind-stuffing that occurred under that regime had the virtue of providing meaningful subject matter—notably history, geography, the sciences, rhetoric, and grammar—and an atmosphere conducive to absorbing it. Humanistic Psychology reduced that subject matter to make room for lessons in self-esteem and self-gratification. To a significant extent, it also changed the teacher from transmitter of knowledge to nonjudgmental "facilitator" and replaced classroom decorum with confusion, if not chaos.

Let's pause and look back at the historical developments we have been discussing. The Enlightenment provoked a dispute that has lasted for the better part of three centuries. At first, Positivism exalted reason and Romanticism denounced it. But then something strange happened: Positivism came to doubt the average person's capacity for reasoning. As a result, the goal of education changed from teaching students *how* to think to telling them *what* to think. The way was then clear for Romanticism to triumph, which it did in the form of Humanistic Psychology.

It would be difficult to overstate the influence of Humanistic Psychology. During the 1960s and 1970s, the movement gave new impetus to Rousseau's ideas that (1) human nature is unqualifiedly good, (2) society is corrupt, (3) morality is subjective, and (4) feelings are more reliable than thought. These ideas provided the theme for self-help publishing and became the principal perspective in the training of psychologists, social caseworkers, guidance counselors, marriage counselors, student personnel professionals, and even spiritual advisors. The same views found their way into many liberal arts, fine arts, and journalism programs, and the graduates of these programs have, in turn, given expression to the views in contemporary movies, television programs, and journalism.

Over the years, there have been challenges to these developments in education, among them two notable efforts to restore the human mind to the learning process—the Great Books movement and the Critical Thinking movement. The former succeeded in establishing some curriculums and even a few institutions devoted to classical education. The latter created courses in critical thinking and provided a wide assortment of teaching materials. But neither succeeded in displacing mind-stuffing in teaching methods, testing, or the major textbooks.

THE CHALLENGE TO YOU

So complete has been Romanticism's success that its central ideas are assumed to be self-evident and are therefore never questioned. That, perhaps, is the best reason to question them. The first two views regarding human nature and society are not our main concern, but a brief comment on each is in order. The idea that human nature is unqualifiedly good is contradicted by half or more of the stories in any evening's newscast, as well as by personal experience; those stories demonstrate that, given the choice between good and evil, people sometimes choose evil. And the only way for the second view to be true—that society is corrupt—is for at least some individuals to be corrupt, because society is nothing more than a collection of individuals. Blaming society serves only to avoid placing responsibility where it belongs.

Rousseau's related argument that children are good until parents and teachers corrupt them conveniently ignores the fact that all parents and teachers were once children. Following Rousseau's logic, they, too, were corrupted by their parents, and the blame must therefore be passed on back through the generations, all the way to our ancestral cave parents or to Adam and Eve, who—it should be noted—blamed the serpent!

We will examine Rousseau's third idea, that morality is subjective, in chapter 7, "Making Ethical Judgments." That leaves the fourth idea, that feelings are more reliable than thought. If this is true, then the banishing of mind from education must be counted a positive development. On the other hand, if feelings are less reliable than thought, following them is a mistake. Which is it? Let's see.

The term *feelings* and its near-synonyms *hunches, urges, impressions, impulses,* and *intuitions* refer to ideas that occur spontaneously, without conscious or controlled mental effort. Some great achievements have been credited to such spontaneity. For example, when the German chemist Kekule, exhausted from his struggle to find the solution to a scientific problem, dozed for a brief time, the solution appeared in a dream. The great German writer Goethe is said to have had a solution to a literary problem appear in similarly dramatic fashion. And the English poet Coleridge reportedly awoke from a dream with 200 to 300 lines of a new poem clearly in mind.

However, thought may be more involved in such events than the Romantics believe. The unconscious mind may simply have completed a process that was begun by the conscious mind.[21] After all, insight favors people who have devoted years to the study of their subjects, not to the uninitiated. Great insights in chemistry don't pop into the minds of accountants, nor do brilliant new surgical procedures occur to bartenders.

Moreover, even a brief reflection on everyday experience will reveal several negative characteristics of feelings. To begin with, they tend to be *capricious*, changing as rapidly as our moods change. Forbearance can turn quickly to impatience, calmness to anger, kindness to cruelty, love to hate, for no good reason. Feelings can also be *deceptive*, leading us to confuse our wishes and hopes with reality. Smokers feel that cigarettes are harmless, sunbathers feel impervious to skin cancer, anorexics feel fat, and people who habitually offend others feel unashamed. In addition, feelings are *manipulable*. When hucksters and demagogues want to take advantage of us by selling us something we don't need or getting us to do something that is not in our interests, they aim for our emotions rather than our intellects.

Do feelings ever prompt us to behave wonderfully? Of course. The problem is, they don't do so consistently enough for us to rely on them. If we were going on a trip through unknown and formidable terrain—a jungle, say, or an inhospitable mountain region—we wouldn't settle a guide who succeeded in getting people back safely half the time. We'd find a guide with a better record. We should do no less with the guide we choose for the important decisions of life. Dozens of times a day, every day of our lives, we need to distinguish wise from unwise responses, helpful from harmful, profitable from unprofitable, prudent from imprudent, ethical from unethical. To do so, we need to assess the situation, consider our options, and make good choices. Only thinking does that. Not perfectly, to be sure, but much more reliably than feelings do.

Thus, the movement that began several centuries ago as a testament to reason and intellect has devolved into a festival of feelings. The great irony is that although nothing matters more to the success and fulfillment of individuals or the longevity of nations than the cultivation of the human mind, the schools and other agencies of modern culture seem oblivious of the fact. Therefore, the challenge of making your mind matter is yours and yours alone. The chapters that follow are designed to help you meet that challenge.

I

UNDERSTANDING THINKING

There are two ways to slide easily through life: to believe everything or to doubt everything; both ways save us from thinking.

—Alfred Korzybski

The business of the mind, as everyone knows, is thinking. But what exactly is thinking? Does all mental activity qualify or should the definition be more restrictive? Are there different kinds of thinking? If so, do they work together? Even more important, what is thinking *for*? What, if anything, is its purpose?

The ancient Romans defined thinking as "shaking ideas together."[a] Albert Einstein regarded it as playfully combining ideas. John Dewey's definition focused on the various *processes* of thinking: "Thinking is inquiry, investigation, turning over, probing or delving into, so as to find something new or to see what is already known in a different light. In short it is questioning." Yet another way of defining thinking is in terms of its *goals*: "Thinking is any mental activity that helps formulate or solve a problem, make a decision, or fulfill a desire to understand. It is a searching for answers, a reaching for meaning."[1]

In all these definitions, thinking is a *purposeful* activity over which we exercise some *control*. Merely being conscious and having words and images floating around in our minds does not constitute thinking, any more than merely sitting behind the wheel of a car with its motor running constitutes

---

[a] The Latin word for thinking was *cogitare*, from which came our English word *cogitate*.

driving. Thinking involves taking control of our mental activity and moving it toward some goal, just as driving involves putting the car in gear and steering our way to a destination. Daydreaming does not qualify as thinking because we are passive spectators to its activity and because its direction is random rather than purposeful.

The raw material of thinking is ideas. An idea consists of a subject and its predicate. Neither "Sally" nor "tax relief" qualifies as an idea, but "Sally still mourns her father's passing" and "Tax reform is needed" both do. Ideas come to us in various ways, the most obvious being our own conscious effort. For example, the thought about Sally could have occurred to you after you noticed her eyes tearing up at the mention of her father's name or walked into her room and saw her staring at his picture. But unless you have made a special study of the tax code, you would probably have gotten the idea about tax reform from someone else, perhaps a member of Congress speaking on a talk show.

It is not surprising that many or even *most* of the ideas in our minds have come from other people. Long before we are able to assess the world for ourselves, we hear our parents' and siblings' assessments of it. When we go to school and learn to read, we are exposed to teachers' and authors' ideas. Throughout our lives, television, radio, popular magazines, advertising, and the Internet provide countless additional ideas.

There is no practical way to prevent other people's ideas from entering your mind except by becoming a hermit, in which case you'd lose more than you'd gain. Nevertheless, you can get to know the ideas that have taken up residence in your mind and determine whether they are true or false, wise or foolish, beneficial or harmful. Whenever an idea moves out from the shadows of your mind and presents itself to you, ask yourself if you have encountered it before and, if so, where. Do this not just with ideas that seem new, but also with familiar ones, including those you cherish. Next, ask whether you are familiar with the evidence for *and against* the idea. If you are not, investigate. (Don't settle for one side's description of the other side—it's likely to be biased, even if their motives are pure.) If your inquiry validates the idea, extend its lease in your mind. Otherwise, evict it.

If questioning familiar ideas seems extreme, consider how an idea becomes familiar. One way is by hearing it expressed; another is by expressing it ourselves. Let's say that last week you heard someone say, "Our freedoms are being stripped away, one by one." Though you didn't have the time to evaluate the idea, it stayed in your mind. Later in the day you said to a friend, "I heard something really troubling earlier today," and proceeded to repeat the idea. Over the next few days you told several over people. Now, a week after you heard the idea, the subject of freedom has come up in conversation and you recall it, not as something you heard someone else say but *as something you said yourself*. If someone disagrees with it, you take the challenge personally and defend the idea as vigorously as you would defend an idea you had examined carefully and validated.

How many untested ideas have you acquired in this way? The only way you'll ever know is by testing familiar ideas as carefully as you test unfamiliar ones. Be especially careful about ideas that are often expressed in the media or that you can't remember having compared with opposing ideas. Over time, this simple approach will greatly improve the quality of your ideas.

BASIC AXIOMS OF THINKING

Every worthwhile activity has its principles and standards drawn from the experiences and insights of generations of knowledgeable people. This is true of sports, the fine arts, science, and mathematics. It is also true of thinking. Unfortunately, the current fashion is to resent all standards other than one's own. (Rousseau lives!) Sometimes this sentiment is indulged in the extreme. Not long ago, I walked up to a United Parcel Service (UPS) counter just as the woman in front of me was finishing an angry rebuke of the clerk. After she stormed out of the building, I asked the clerk what the problem was. She explained that a few days earlier the woman had brought in a package with the mailing address in the upper left corner and her return address just below and to the right of center. At that time, the clerk had politely explained that this placement was nonstandard and would be confusing to the UPS routing and delivery people.

"I don't care what your standard is," the woman had snorted. "This is the way I do it."

I then asked the clerk, "What was she upset about today?"

The clerk responded, "She was complaining because the UPS driver just delivered the package to her instead of to the person she was sending it to."

Given the current fashions of preferring emotion to thought and rejecting standards set by others, no axiom in any subject is likely to receive universal acceptance. This fact underscores the importance of judging the following axioms by the weight of the evidence rather than by their popularity or familiarity.

Axiom 1: Truth Is Objective rather than Subjective, and Discovered rather than Created

The opposite view is more popular today. Many people no longer speak of *"the* truth," only *"my* truth" or *"your* truth." They believe that the very act of regarding an idea as true *makes it true.*

The popular view is comforting in its assurance that no one is ever wrong about anything. But imagine what the world would be like if everyone accepted it and lived by it. Teachers would be free to assign whatever grades they chose, regardless of students' performance. If a student protested, "You took off credit for my *correct* answers and that's not fair," the teacher would say "What is correct or fair to you is not necessarily correct or fair to me . . . and I have the grade book."

Suppose that a careless driver smashed into your parked car and demolished it. If the matter went to court and the driver claimed that your parked car *had caused the accident,* what would you say? If you protested that his claim was absurd, he would answer, "According to my truth, it's perfectly reasonable." (The judge's decision would depend on his or her "truth," whatever that might happen to be.) Criminal cases couldn't be tried, because everyone would swear to tell "MY truth, MY whole truth, and nothing but MY truth" and the jury would have no basis for deciding guilt or innocence.

It gets worse. If everyone really believed that truth is created rather than discovered, research in every discipline would grind to a halt. How many historians would spend their days poring over dusty old diaries? How many archaeologists would travel across the world to forsaken places that lack sanitation and air conditioning? How many medical researchers would bother with laborious laboratory tasks? Very few, indeed. The sensible ones would dream up an answer to whatever question they were addressing, file their report, and head for the golf course.

So far, the axiom is proving more reasonable than the popular belief. Let's consider a few actual cases and see if this assessment is confirmed:

- In the early seventeenth century, Galileo shocked the world by saying that the Earth revolves around the sun. At that time, virtually everyone else believed that the sun revolves around the Earth. Is it more reasonable to say that Galileo created an idea that was true for him but not necessarily for others or that he discovered an objective truth that was the same for everyone? Clearly the latter. The relationship between Earth and sun is one physical reality, so there can be only one correct answer.

- For several hundred years, the painting entitled *The Man with the Golden Helmet* was believed to be the work of the Dutch master Rembrandt. Then, in the 1990s, scientists proved that it was the work of another artist. Surely it makes more sense to say that the traditional belief was false and truth has finally been discovered than to say that both beliefs are true.

- When jazz musician Billy Tipton died at age seventy-four, it was learned that "he" was actually a woman. Tipton had begun the deception early in life to increase "his" chances as a musician. Virtually everyone who knew "him," including "his" three adopted sons, was certain "he" was a man. Did people's believing that Tipton was a man make that idea true? Did the person who performed the autopsy *create* Tipton's actual identity? No to both questions. There was a single truth. For a time it was hidden and then it was discovered.

As British statesman Winston Churchill once said, "The truth is incontrovertible; panic may resent it; ignorance may deride it; malice may distort it, but there it is." Churchill was not saying that we possess all truths or that they are easy to grasp; obviously, much remains unknown about every subject and many truths are complex. He was suggesting only that the truth cannot be shaped to fit our preferences and we do our minds a disservice to pretend otherwise.

Axiom 2: If Two Statements Are Mutually Contradictory, One Must Be False

"Mutually contradictory" means that each statement negates the other. No doubt you learned in school that during World War II the Nazis murdered nine million people. The horrible events of that time are known as the Holocaust. But you may not have heard that some authors categorically deny that those events occurred. (Those authors even claim that the photographs of piles of bodies were fabricated.) The two views completely contradict each other—either the Holocaust happened or it did not. It cannot have partly happened any more than a woman can be partly pregnant or a man can be sort of dead.[b]

Whenever you encounter completely contradictory viewpoints on an issue, the appropriate response is to investigate and find out which view is

---

[b] The viewpoint that the numbers murdered have been exaggerated or that some of the stories have been fabricated is not a third position on the issue. It merely adds a qualification to "It happened."

correct before proceeding. Any attempt to reconcile the irreconcilable can only add confusion and prolong the controversy. Unfortunately, such attempts are fairly common and they often create suspicion and animosity.

The most obvious example in our time concerns the abortion controversy, in which one side claims that the fetus is a human being and the other says it is not. Failing to realize that the two views are incompatible, many people have proposed a compromise—making abortion "safe but rare." This well-intentioned effort was doomed to failure. If a fetus is a human being, the safety of the procedure to the woman is irrelevant; if a fetus is not a human being, there is no reason to make abortion rare. The question that cries out to be fairly and honestly addressed is, "Is a fetus a human being?"[c]

There is another side to this axiom—sometimes two statements that *appear* to be mutually contradictory are *not really so.* In such cases, you do not have to choose between them. Instead you can accept both, each in its own way. Consider these maxims: "Look before you leap" and "He who hesitates is lost." At first thought, each seems to negate the other, but in fact they are compatible—we can act quickly without acting mindlessly. The same may be said of the maxims, "Many hands make light work" and "Too many cooks spoil the broth." A job does go faster when many people work together, as long as all work cooperatively. An example of such cooperative activity is an Amish barn raising.

The ability to tell when middle ground exists between opposing ideas and when it does not is an important aspect of effective thinking.

Axiom 3: The Human Mind Is Fallible

Few axioms are as easily documented as this one. Research on perception reveals that we sometimes see what we want or expect to see rather than what is before us. The classic study, many times replicated, was conducted by William Stern. He staged a confrontation in a large classroom. Two actors entered at the front of the room and began to exchange angry words. Eventually one of them drew a handgun. At that point, Stern ended the incident and asked the class to write a thorough description of what they had just witnessed. Most were wrong about most of the details, including what was said, who said it, and the description of the weapon.[2]

---

[c] The answer to that question would not necessarily end the controversy over abortion. For example, if the fetus were found to be a human being, another issue would arise: *Should the law treat the fetus as a person with the same constitutional rights enjoyed by other persons?* That issue would also have to be resolved.

Even when we perceive accurately, our later recall of the event may be flawed. Memory research reveals that memory does not work like a DVD, with every image and sound permanently and unchangeably recorded. Memory is typically a mixture of what we perceived at the time, later knowledge and interpretation derived from other people as well as our own thoughts, and our present attitudes and emotions.[3] This is not to say that all our memories are inaccurate, only that memory is imperfect and our confidence in its accuracy is often misplaced.

Human judgment is also imperfect. Whether our mental mistakes are caused by inadequate information, overactive imagination, or just careless thinking, they are numerous and often costly. Headaches were once thought to be caused by demons inside the skull and treatments ranged from boring holes in the skull to let the demons out to drinking potions made from cow's brain, goat dung, or beaver testicles. The heart was long considered the seat of consciousness. Women were considered incapable of strenuous mental activity. As late as 1900, marijuana, heroin, and morphine were all available over the counter at corner drugstores. According to one pharmacist of that era, "Heroin clears the complexion, gives buoyancy to the mind, regulates the stomach and the bowels, and is, in fact, a perfect guardian of health."

The greatest inaccuracies in judgment occur in predictions of the future, as the following examples illustrate:[4]

- When the railroad was invented, a London professor declared, "Rail travel at high speed is not possible because passengers, unable to breathe, would die of asphyxia." The speed he was referring to was about 25 MPH.
- Sir John Eric Erichsen, a famous British surgeon, predicted in 1837 that surgery would never be performed on the abdomen, the chest, or the brain.
- In 1900, the president of the British Royal Society pronounced X-rays to be "a hoax."
- In 1899, the commissioner of the U.S. Patent Office recommended that the office be abolished because "Everything that can be invented has been invented."
- In 1955, *Variety Magazine* said of the new rock and roll music: "It will be gone by June."

Remembering that your mind is imperfect will help you be more careful in your thinking and thereby reduce the number and the foolishness of your errors.

Axiom 4: Ideas Have Consequences

Somehow, it has become popular to believe that ideas cannot hurt anyone. "No one was ever assaulted by an idea" is a common expression, usually made in the defense of "objectionable" themes and treatments, notably sex and violence, in literature and films. People who harbor this notion may think they are demonstrating respect for ideas, but they are actually disparaging and trivializing ideas. After all, if ideas can't hurt us, they can't help us either, in which case they have little value. And if they have little value, there's no point in making an effort to distinguish between practical and impractical, logical and illogical, or wise and foolish ideas.

In reality, however, ideas have considerable power to help and hurt. They are the driving force—the engines, if you will—of our actions. The idea that a stock is going to depreciate in value causes investors to sell. The idea that a nation is under serious threat of attack leads to military mobilization. And the idea that someone is gossiping behind your back will alter your attitude toward that person.

Some years ago, while conducting educational seminars in Singapore, I had occasion to visit a number of schools and interact with children of various ages. I immediately noticed how respectful they were toward adults. When adults spoke to them, they looked and listened intently. When asked a question, they answered thoughtfully. When given opportunity and encouragement to ask questions, they did so politely. This behavior was very different from what I was used to observing in American students. And the difference, I am convinced, was that their culture did a much better job of promoting the idea that teachers (and parents) are worthy of respect and even admiration.

Another experience in Singapore was equally revealing. I was standing with a Singaporean colleague at a busy downtown intersection. Dozens of people lined both sides of the street waiting for the light to change. When I realized that not a single person was jaywalking, I asked my colleague why. He explained that the police issued tickets for jaywalking and the newspapers published the names of offenders, adding that having one's name presented in a negative light would bring shame to one's family, and no one wanted to do that.

Psychiatrist Thomas Szasz traces the modern belief that people are not responsible for their behavior largely to Sigmund Freud's idea that free will does not exist. Szasz notes that "although an entire volume of the *Standard Edition* of Freud's collected works is devoted to an index, there is no entry for *responsibility* in it."[5] Similarly, Judith Reisman has traced the current problem of pedophilia to the idea that early sexual experience, including adult-child contact, is emotionally healthy, an idea she finds in Alfred Kinsey's writings and in *Playboy* magazine.[6]

The more you appreciate the power of ideas to influence behavior and, thereby, create or solve human problems, the more motivated you will be to think analytically.

THE DIMENSIONS OF THINKING

Thinking has three broad dimensions: reflective, creative, and critical. Our knowledge of the first and third come from the field of philosophy; our knowledge of the creative dimension comes from the field of psychology. Because two separate disciplines are involved, our knowledge of thinking is not as well integrated as it might be. The creative dimension tends to be associated exclusively with problem solving; the critical, exclusively with issue analysis; and the reflective dimension tends to be neglected in both activities. This lack of integration is unfortunate because all three dimensions play a role in virtually every mental challenge. Let's look closely at each and then consider how they work in combination.

The Reflective Dimension

Reflection *identifies challenges and opportunities* and deepens our understanding of everyday experiences. The essential element in reflection is curiosity. Almost every child is curious about people, places, and things. "Why, Mommy?" and "Why, Daddy?" are among the most common expressions of young children. Not coincidentally, people acquire more knowledge at this stage of life than at any other. Unfortunately, parents soon grow tired of answering their children's questions and most teachers have too many students and too many prescribed lessons to indulge students' curiosity. Eventually, children stop asking questions; many even stop thinking of questions to ask.

Fortunately, curiosity can be regained by cultivating the habit of reflection. To do so, make time each day for reflecting on the experiences of the past twelve or twenty-four hours. Fifteen minutes a day is enough, though a half-hour is better. The evening is probably the best time because the day's events are most easily remembered then, but if you are an early riser, the morning might be more convenient. Begin by reviewing significant events of the previous twenty-four hours and asking relevant questions about each. Here are some examples:

- If you encountered a problem that took time to solve or that you weren't able to solve, ask how the problem arose, whether it was new or recurrent, who besides you was affected by it, and what might have caused it.

- If you experienced dissatisfaction, frustration, or annoyance, ask what about the situation bothered you, whether the condition was new or recurring, and what changes in the situation would make you react differently.

- If you were involved in or witnessed a discussion of a controversial issue, ask what view each person expressed, what evidence or reasoning he or she offered to support it, how each person reacted to the other · view(s), whether any agreement was reached, and whether a compromise view is possible.

- If someone said something you hadn't ever heard expressed in quite the same way before and that you found interesting, ask what about the statement aroused your interest, what its implications might be for your life or the lives of people you know, and where you might learn more about the subject.

- If you thought, said, or did something that proved to be unwise or unproductive, ask what alternative approaches were open to you and what outcomes each might have produced.

- If you reacted to a person or situation in a way that left you feeling displeased with yourself, ask why you reacted as you did, whether you have reacted that way in the past, and how else you might have reacted. Consider not only reactions that you expressed outwardly but also those that you kept to yourself.

Your daily periods of reflection will help you to identify the problems and issues that deserve closer attention. The questions you ask about them will become the basis for gathering information and applying creative and critical thinking.

When you begin to develop the habit of reflection, you will no doubt find yourself becoming more observant at times other than your daily reflective period. As a result, you will begin to notice in everyday experience many details that would otherwise escape your attention.[d] And the more you notice, the more fruitful your later reflection is likely to be.

---

[d] If you have a sense of humor, some of your observations will make you laugh. For example, you may notice, as George Carlin did, how odd it is that people sing "Take Me Out to the Ball Game" when they are already there and that they push the remote buttons harder when they know the batteries are dead.

The Creative Dimension

This dimension of thinking *produces* ideas that solve problems and re-solve issues. Until the mid-twentieth century, creativity was shrouded in mystery. Since then, however, research has produced many insights and exploded a number of myths. For example, it is now known that creativity requires neither high IQ nor special talent, that alcohol and drugs hinder rather than enhance creative performance, and that creativity is a sign of mental health rather than mental instability. It is recognized, too, that bizarre behavior engaged in for its own sake is not a form of creativity.[e]

The more ideas you produce in response to a problem or issue, the better the chance you will have some good ideas. The reason many people are idea-poor is that they settle for the first idea that comes to mind. Often as not, the first idea has little to recommend it besides familiarity. In rare cases, it might actually be a superior idea, but the only way that can be determined is by comparing it with a broad range of alternative ideas.

Before we discuss techniques for thinking creatively, we must clarify the difference between a problem and an issue. A *problem* is a condition that is regarded as unacceptable; an *issue* is a matter about which informed people disagree. The essential difference is that an issue is by definition controversial, whereas a problem is not.[f] Thus, a problem is solved by finding a way to change the situation for the better; an issue is resolved (overcome) by determining which view is most reasonable. Because of this difference, the application of creative thinking is somewhat different for problems and issues, so we will so we will discuss each separately.

Problems.   The best format for expressing a problem is the "How can?" format. Suppose you are the manager of a company cafeteria and you have received many complaints about the slowness of the service, particularly during peak hours. One expression of the problem would be "How can I persuade my superiors to enlarge the cafeteria?" That would yield at best a few meager ideas, none of which would have much of a chance of succeeding, so you might also ask, "How can I improve the traffic flow?" "How can I reduce the time it takes to fill each order?" and "How can I speed up the check-out process?" This would give you four different avenues of thought, each leading to different kinds of solutions to the problem.

---

[e] George F. Kneller made a similar point about creativity in the arts, noting that "uninhibited swiveling at the hips is hardly creative dancing, nor is hurling colors at a canvas creative painting."

[f] A particular solution to a problem may, however, be controversial.

Next, you would answer each "How can?" question. Because the first answer to each is likely to be a familiar, common idea, you would strive for numerous answers. You would also postpone judgment of the ideas until the critical thinking stage because the act of judging interrupts the flow of ideas. If, despite postponing judgment, your flow of ideas is little more than a trickle, you can stimulate your imagination with one or more of these approaches:

Force uncommon responses. After you have written down the ideas that come effortlessly, say to yourself, "So much for the common ideas. Now I am going to produce some uncommon ones." Then try to think of possible solutions you have not considered before or heard others express. This approach takes a bit of daring because it requires you to stray from the familiar and comfortable—but it is not as difficult as it may seem.

Use analogy. An analogy is a reference to a similarity between two otherwise different things. Galileo got the idea for the pendulum after sitting in church and watching a chandelier swinging. Gutenberg got the idea for the printing press after visiting a winery and watching the vintners use a winepress. The inventor of the forklift truck got his insight after watching steel fingers flipping doughnuts in a bakery. To use analogy, ask what the problem situation is like, what it reminds you of.

Visualize the solution. This technique is an effective way of identifying possible solutions to problems. Let's say you manage a hotel and people are complaining that the elevators are too slow. Your first idea is to add elevators, but the cost would be prohibitive. So you try to visualize the solution by closing your eyes and imagining people waiting *patiently* for the elevators. Wondering what is different in this case, you "look" more closely at the scene and "see" that they are looking in mirrors mounted next to and between the elevators. "That's it," you decide. "I'll put up mirrors and distract them so that the wait doesn't seem so long." (Incidentally, this solution was reportedly adopted some years ago in a Texas office building.)

Issues.   Issues are expressed by turning each point of controversy into a question prefaced by "is," "does," "would," or "should." The points of controversy can easily be established by examining the assertions made by people on either side of the issue.

A current issue concerns the issuance of school vouchers to parents of students in underperforming inner-city schools. The vouchers, worth between $2,500 and $5,000 each, could be used to defray the tuition costs of private or parochial schools. Supporters of voucher systems claim they give poor parents the same choice in education that wealthier Americans enjoy. They also argue that, if widely adopted, voucher programs would motivate public school teachers and administrators to improve the quality of their programs so that parents would want their children to remain in public school. Opponents charge that voucher programs are in violation of the principle of separation of church and state and drain necessary resources, causing public school education to decline further.

Here is how you would use these claims and counterclaims to frame the issue: *Do voucher programs give poor parents the shame choice in education that wealthier Americans enjoy? Would voucher programs, if widely adopted, motivate the public schools to improve the quality of their teaching? Are voucher programs in violation of the principle of separation of church and state? Do voucher programs drain away necessary resources from public schools?* Only by raising and answering such questions can you develop an informed opinion on whether vouchers are a good idea. And you should have an informed opinion about vouchers before asking "How can I implement a voucher system?" Thus, where controversy exists, it should be resolved before problem solving begins.

One or both sides of a dispute will often make more claims than this. In that case, you would frame the additional claims as questions. By investigating and finding the answers to each of the questions, you would produce many of the ideas needed to resolve the issue. Although this activity requires less imagination that the approaches used to solve problems, the following techniques provide an opportunity to use your imagination:

Think of additional questions. It sometimes happens that certain aspects of an issue are so controversial and the opposing views so strong that other aspects, including some equally important ones, tend to be ignored. In the case of school vouchers, you might ask, "Where vouchers have been tried, did the students who used them improve their academic performance?" "In the voucher programs that have been tried, were the vouchers issued to the parents or to the school?" (This question has a bearing on the church/state separation question.) "Has any similar program been tried in American education and, if so, was it successful?" In researching this question, you would find that the G.I. Bill enabled many World War II and Korean War veterans to receive a college education. This fact, however, would raise another question: "Is a college 'voucher' program really comparable to a K–12 voucher program?"

Imagine scenarios that illuminate the issue. Scenarios are situations or events relevant to the issue. Consider a different issue: that of whether the courts should eliminate some "exclusionary rules." These are the rules under which evidence is excluded from a trial if it was inappropriately obtained—for example, without a properly executed search warrant or without the accused perpetrator being apprised of his rights. Here are a few of the many possible scenarios you might imagine and the lines of thought each might suggest.

- A man is in the process of being arrested for murder. Before the police have a chance to read him his rights, he blurts out, "I did it and I'm glad. He [the victim] insulted me one time too many." *Line of thought: perhaps freely volunteered information such as this should be admissible in court even though the man had not been read his rights.*
- After being interrogated for twelve hours by a team of detectives and told he will not be allowed to make a phone call until he confesses to having raped a woman, a suspect signs a prepared statement. *Line of thought: perhaps the confession should be excluded in such coercive circumstances.*
- After a robbery has occurred in an apartment house, two detectives are knocking on doors to determine if neighbors saw or heard anything helpful to the investigation. They knock on one door, a woman lets them in, and while one detective is speaking to her, the other casually flips open a basket on her coffee table and sees a large bag of marijuana. They confiscate it and arrest her. *Line of thought: On the one hand, she invited them in. On the other hand, she didn't give the detective permission to open the basket. Which fact is more significant?*

Even these few examples demonstrate how imagined scenarios can deepen your understanding of issues, particularly more subtle aspects, and give you additional ideas to consider. Of course, such scenarios should be used to supplement actual cases rather than replace them.

The Critical Dimension

We have seen that reflective thinking identifies the challenges and opportunities that warrant closer examination and that creative thinking produces a variety of ideas in response to those challenges and issues. The third dimension is critical thinking and it is the most misunderstood. Some people regard it as a negative activity, a more formal variety of nitpicking. No doubt this is because the word "critical" is sometimes used in the sense of "overly judgmental." In reality, however, critical thinking is a positive activity, the purpose of which is to *evaluate* the ideas produced by creative thinking and identify the best one. Without critical thinking, we would have an assortment of competing ideas and no way to choose among them.

Another common misconception is that critical thinking is appropriately directed toward other people's ideas but never toward our own. In reality, our ideas need evaluation as much as other people's because our minds, like other people's, are prone to errors of perception, memory, and judgment. In failing to examine our own ideas critically, we deprive ourselves of a chance to improve and refine them.

Because critical thinking is, in several respects, more complex than reflective and creative thinking, our discussion of it requires more space than a single section of one chapter. Accordingly, we will merely identify the various aspects of critical thinking here and leave our discussion of them for subsequent chapters.[g]

Overcoming obstacles to effective thinking.   Certain mental habits and attitudes prevent us from thinking well. It is important to know what those habits and attitudes are and, if we have acquired them, to replace them with ones that enhance rather than hinder our thinking.

Resisting manipulation.   Contrary to a currently popular notion, independence of mind does not come automatically but must be achieved. The way to achieve it is to understand how manipulation occurs and how to avoid falling victim to it.

Testing ideas.   Essential to critical thinking are the ability to distinguish between statements of fact and statements of opinion and skill in testing the quality of each.

Recognizing errors in reasoning.   Mistakes in reasoning come in many varieties and can occur quite easily. By becoming familiar with them, we can lessen their occurrence and more effectively correct them.

Analyzing arguments.   An argument is a *presentation* a person makes for his or her viewpoint.[h] Such a presentation typically explains the line of thought by which the person reached the conclusion. Thinking critically about an argument entails examining the truth of the statements, the amount and quality of the evidence, and the logic of the person's reasoning. In order to conduct this examination, we need to know the kinds of errors that might occur and to be skilled in detecting them.

Making ethical judgments.   Ethical issues pose a special challenge because they demand, in addition to the usual production and evaluation of ideas, the application of criteria specific to ethics.

THE WISE APPROACH TO THINKING

So far in this chapter, the focus has been on the fundamentals of thinking: the axioms that provide the foundation for the effective use of the mind, the different dimensions of thinking and their distinguishing characteristics, and the role each dimension plays in problem solving and decision making.

---

[g] The content of the remaining chapters will, of course, also be relevant to the other dimensions of thinking.

[h] Another meaning of argument, which does not concern us here, is the *process* by which two (or more) people exchange viewpoints on an issue, usually with the intention of persuading each other.

Now we will turn to a more practical concern—the consolidation of all that knowledge into a simple yet effective *strategy* for meeting everyday thinking challenges. It is called the WISE approach. (WISE is an acronym that stands for Wonder, Investigate, Speculate, and Evaluate.[7])

WONDER: Pay close attention to your everyday experiences and your reactions to them. Review both at least once a day and ask which challenges represent problems and issues that deserve closer, individual attention.

INVESTIGATE: Decide what information you need to solve the problem or resolve the issue. Then consult authoritative sources in the library or on the Internet to obtain that information.

SPECULATE: Ask questions that open up various lines of thought. Use "how can?" questions for problems and "is?" "does?" or "should?" problems for issues. (Look back at "The Creative Dimension" if you need to refresh your memory.) Then produce as many answers as you can for each question. Each of these answers will represent or suggest a solution to the problem or a viewpoint on the issue.

EVALUATE: Test the possible solutions or viewpoints and determine which is most effective and/or reasonable. If necessary, combine elements of two or three solutions or viewpoints to form a new one.

2

OVERCOMING OBSTACLES

Either you control your mental habits and attitudes, or they control you.
The choice is yours.

Chapter 1 discussed the purpose of thinking and the axioms that provide its foundation, as well as the various dimensions of thinking—reflective, creative, critical—and the role each plays in problem solving and decision making. It also outlined a comprehensive approach, the WISE approach, to problems and issues. Acquiring this knowledge is an essential first step to excellence in thinking. But since thinking is a skill, knowledge alone is not enough. You must also become proficient in *applying* your knowledge. However, given the schools' neglect of thinking and mass culture's preference for feeling, you might have developed certain habits and associated attitudes that hinder such application. In this chapter, we will identify those habits and attitudes and explore ways to overcome them.

THE BASIC PROBLEM: EGOCENTRISM

British historian Arnold Toynbee described egocentrism as "the prison of [our] inborn selfishness" and "the fundamental problem" that every great religion and philosophy has been concerned with overcoming.[1] The difficulty in overcoming egocentrism is partly explained by the fact that most of

us are inclined to see it as characteristic of other people but not of ourselves. Egocentrism is expressed in four ways: mine-is-better perspective,
self-serving bias, inflated self-esteem, and face saving.

Mine-Is-Better Perspective

This perspective is the most obvious expression of egocentrism. Small
children say, "My mommy is prettier than any other mommy" or "My daddy
is bigger and stronger." They also make similar statements about their
houses, toys, and finger paintings. All such statements say, in effect, "Everything that is mine is better *because it is mine.*" As people get older, they
generally stop making such statements, but they continue to harbor that belief, particularly about matters they consider important, such race, religion,
ethnic group, social class, and political party.[a] A mine-is-better outlook is
also commonly found in matters of opinion—compatible viewpoints are
considered reasonable and even brilliant; opposing viewpoints, absurd.

People are often unaware of their mine-is-better outlook because it
works at the level of assumption rather than of thought. In other words,
people who have such an outlook don't *reason* that people like themselves
are superior people; they merely take for granted that they are and behave accordingly, warmly welcoming people they identify with and dis-
playing suspicion or distrust toward others. The same reaction exists toward ideas. One writer described a typical mine-is-better reaction of a
group he once belonged to: "The point was, we didn't have to be told—
we knew what a fascist was. A hater. A moral abomination. One opposed
to everything good and decent and right. *Someone who disagreed with
us*"[2] (emphasis added). People who assume that their viewpoint is better
than all others are unable to see their own errors and to profit from other
people's insights. As a result, they seldom grow in understanding or improve their mental proficiency.

You may not be able to eliminate your mine-is-better outlook entirely,
but you can learn to control it. Start by acknowledging that no one, including you, is completely right all the time and that it is in your best interest to
find out when you are mistaken. After all, there is no shame in changing
your mind, but there is in clinging stubbornly to shallow or mistaken ideas.
Then, whenever you encounter other viewpoints, set aside any assumptions
and give them a fair hearing.

---

[a] When egocentrism is extended to one's group, it is called *ethno*centrism.

Self-Serving Bias

This expression of egocentrism is related to mine-is-better perspective and is defined as the habit of perceiving, remembering, and interpreting events in a way that is complimentary to us, even when such interpretations are unjustified. The existence of this habit has long been noted in social psychology.[3] One kind of self-serving bias is "attribut[ing] the behavior of others to personality factors and that of ourselves to situational factors."[4] For example, if Mary and I have an argument and behave in exactly the same manner, I may say that she is an aggressive person whereas I was merely defending my point of view. If Arthur forgets my birthday, he is insensitive and uncaring; if I forget his, it's because I've been unusually busy at work lately.

This may seem to be merely a language game, but it is often more than that. Self-serving bias can affect our perception in much the same way that a flawed eyeglass lens distorts vision. So we might really perceive that our failures are someone else's fault and our successes redound to our credit. Studies have shown that some people, when reading data that support their beliefs, perceive it to be much more substantial and persuasive than data that challenge their beliefs.[5] Some people will even go so far as to condemn books they haven't read—in their minds, any book that challenges their belief *must* be wrong.

The ability to perceive events clearly and accurately is obviously necessary for effective thinking, so it is in your interest to overcome any tendency you have to self-serving bias.

Inflated Self-Esteem

If you have accepted the fashionable notion that most people suffer from low self-esteem, need constant reminders of how wonderful they are, and are emotionally damaged by criticism, you will be surprised to learn that this notion is a myth.

Thomas Gilovich notes that "one of the most documented findings in psychology is that the average person purports to believe extremely flattering things about himself or herself, beliefs that do not stand up to objective reality." For example, "a large majority of the general public thinks that they are more intelligent, more fair-minded, less prejudiced, and more skilled behind the wheel of an automobile than the average person." Gilovich also cites a survey of a million high school students in which 70 percent judged themselves above average in leadership ability and only 2 percent classified themselves as below average. Similarly, all the students thought themselves above average in ability to get along with others, 60 percent rated themselves in the top 10 percent, and 25 percent rated themselves in the top 1 percent. (Students are not the only ones with inflated self-images. Gilovich cites a study of university professors, in which 94 percent judged themselves better at their jobs than their colleagues.[6])

But what about all the harm supposedly done by a deficiency of self-esteem, you may wonder. Research psychologist Martin Seligman notes that "there are almost no findings that self-esteem causes anything at all. Rather, self-esteem is caused by a whole panoply of successes and failures. . . . What needs improving is not self-esteem but improvement of our skills [for dealing] with the world."[7] In the view of Alfred Binet, a pioneer in the study of intelligence, one of the most important of those skills is self-criticism.[8] Another researcher, and former director of the U.S. Office of Education's gifted education division, Dorothy A. Sisk, notes that gifted people are more critical of themselves than the average person.[9]

A 1989 international study of math competency and self-image about math performance provides further documentation that self-esteem is no substitute for skill. American participants rated highest in self-assessment and lowest in competency. In contrast, Korean participants rated lowest in self-assessment and highest in competency. Reflecting on this and similar findings, psychologist Paul Vitz observes, "It makes no sense for students to be full of self esteem if they are empty of knowledge," because one day, they will have to face the reality that the praise has been false and the ignorance real.[10]

Face Saving

Yet another expression of egocentrism is face saving—that is, covering up or explaining away our mistakes rather than acknowledging them, at least to ourselves. The dynamic of face saving is perhaps best expressed in the Yiddish proverb, "The girl who can't dance says the band can't play." That hypothetical girl will not be motivated to learn how to dance. Nor are individuals who are afraid of damaging their self-image or the image they project to others likely to seize opportunities to learn and improve themselves.

Just how foolish people can be in their attempts to save face is illustrated by a hoax perpetrated by three Southern California professors of medicine on their colleagues. The professors paid a professional actor to lecture three groups of educators. Armed with a fake identity, "Dr. Myron L. Fox of the Albert Einstein University," false but impressive credentials, and a scholarly sounding topic, "Mathematical Game Theory as Applied to Physical Education," the actor proceeded to make one meaningless, conflicting statement after another. His words were a combination of double-talk and academic jargon. During the question-and-answer period, he made even less sense. Yet not one of the fifty-five educators in the audience realized they had been tricked. Some even praised the imposter in this manner: "Excellent presentation, enjoyed listening." "Has warm manner and lively examples." "Is extremely articulate." Evidently, their fear of being thought ignorant prevented them from acknowledging the obvious.[b]

To overcome the tendency to face saving, remind yourself that only by acknowledging a shortcoming will you be motivated to overcome it.

OTHER HABITS THAT OBSTRUCT THOUGHT

The various expressions of ethnocentrism are not the only obstacles to effective thinking. Other important ones are mental sloth, gullibility and conformity, bias for the majority or the minority, bias for or against change, preconceptions, and overreliance on feelings. Let's examine each.

Mental Sloth

This habit consists simply of speaking or acting without thinking. Everyday experience can provide numerous examples, ranging from the comic to the tragic. Here are some typical ones:

- Police in Radnor, Pennsylvania, interrogated a suspect by placing a metal colander on his head and connecting it with wires to a photocopy machine. The message "He's lying" was placed in the copier, and police pressed the copy button each time they thought the suspect wasn't telling the truth. Believing the "lie detector" was working, the suspect confessed. Surely the suspect had seen a colander and a photocopy machine before. Had he been thinking, the attempted deception should have been obvious to him.
- When the railroad killer later identified as Rafael Resendez-Ramirez was being sought, a reporter asked the FBI agent in charge of the

---

[b] The unfortunate effects of face saving are observable at the national, as well as the individual, level. Countries that blame their internal problems, such as poverty and illiteracy, on other nations rather than on the failure of their political and economic systems tend to seek revenge rather than meaningful solutions.

search whether the focus on Hispanics constituted discrimination. The FBI agent politely replied that the description the bureau had received was of an Hispanic male, so it seemed reasonable to look for an Hispanic male.

- Sign on the bottom of a delicatessen dessert: "Do not turn upside down!" A notice on a can of peanuts: "Warning: contains nuts." Another nutty one on an airline's packets of nuts: "Instructions: Open packet, eat nuts."
- Lawyer questioning a woman on the witness stand: "You said the date of conception of (the baby) was August 8th. What were you doing at that time?"
- A: physician-witness replying to another lawyer's foolish question:
  Q: Do you recall the time that you examined the body?
  A: The autopsy started around 8:30 P.M.
  Q: And Mr. Dennington was dead at the time?
  A: No, he was sitting on the table wondering why I was doing an autopsy.
- Spuds Mackenzie, a dog in a beer commercial some years ago, reportedly received 5,000 letters a month, presumably from people expecting him to answer.

Gullibility/Conformity

To be gullible is to be easily deceived. An unusually good example of gullibility occurred a few years ago in Tampa, Florida. A woman was dining alone in a restaurant. A stranger came to her table and told her he just inherited $47 million but needed $250,000 to pay certain fees. She proceeded to lend him that amount without a promissory note. He later asked for another $98,000, promising to double the entire amount she had given him. Again she complied. Then to her surprise, but probably not to yours, he absconded. (The story came out only later, after he was caught.)

To conform is to go along with what others think, say, and do, rather than thinking, speaking, and acting for ourselves. Research reveals that the tendency to conform is common, and often strong enough to lead to ridiculous behavior. For example, in a well-known experiment devised by Solomon Asch, eight students entered the professor's laboratory. Seven were in league with the professor; the eighth was the unknowing subject of the experiment. The group was shown four lines on an otherwise blank page. The students were then asked to decide which of the three lower lines (identified as "A," "B," and "C") matched the top line in length. Line "A" was exactly the same length as the top line, ten inches. The other lines were much shorter or longer. Each of the seven collaborators, in turn, gave the wrong answer, and the pressure mounted on the unknowing subject. When he or she was asked, the choice was clear—give the obviously right answer and stand alone or the wrong answer and enjoy the support of the group. How many subjects denied the testimony of their own eyes in order to fit in with the group? *Four out of every five!*

Bias for the Majority or Minority

Bias may be defined as leaning or tilting toward a group or point of view. If you are biased toward the majority, you will feel more comfortable on the majority side of issues and in time may even assume that the majority view is necessarily the right view. On the other hand, if you tend to be cantankerous, you may enjoy siding with the minority. For example, you may support third-party candidates in elections or take extreme views on social issues.

The problem with being biased for either side is that it prevents you from approaching people and ideas fairly and objectively. Whether the majority or the minority view is right depends on the particulars of the issue, and the only way to make a responsible determination is to give each side a fair hearing.

Bias for or against Change

It has been jokingly said of liberals that they never met a new idea they didn't like, and of conservatives that they never met a new idea they *did* like. Each observation contains an element of truth. Some people are biased for change. They welcome new ideas and new ways of doing things, regarding them as a sign of progress. Anything that is rooted in the past—old methods, old beliefs, old customs and values—they regard as irrelevant. Other people have an equally strong bias against change. To them, the past is sacred and the new, the different, is at best suspect.

Historically, bias against change has created more problems than bias for change. The list of wonderful inventions that were resisted merely because they were new is depressingly long. It includes the plow, the sewing machine, the steam engine, the typewriter, the airplane, and innumerable scientific and medical insights. However, the rapid rate of technological change in our day has shifted the advantage to the opposite bias. Many people think that every new idea is automatically better than the one it is intended to replace.

The problem is that change is neither always good nor always bad. Some new ideas are clearly better than the ones they replace, yet others create more problems than they solve. One example is drugs that are rushed to market before their harmful side effects are identified. Another, more closely related to the subject of this book, is the replacement of mind-building with mind-stuffing that occurred in twentieth-century education.

The way to determine the quality of any new idea is to assess its advantages and disadvantages, and that can be done only if you control your bias for or against change.

Preconceptions

Some years ago, there was a movement to teach the African American dialect known as Ebonics as a second language in California schools. One critic of the proposal wrote as follows: "In plain talk, 'Ebonics' is no more than African-American gutter slang. . . . If Ebonics has any credibility at all, it is as the dialect of the street—the dialect of the pimp, the idiom of the gang-banger and the street thug, the jargon of the school dropout, a form of pidgin English that reeks of African-American failure."[11]

What is your first reaction to this quotation? Do you picture a white racist filled with animosity toward African Americans? A person whose viewpoint is so rooted in hate that it is unworthy of your consideration? If so, you harbor the preconception that all African Americans have the same viewpoint about matters concerning race. That preconception, like so many others, happens to be a *mis*conception. African Americans have a variety of views about matters concerning race. In fact, the author of the above quotation is a well-known African American talk-show host.

As the term implies, preconceptions are notions we have in mind about people and points of view before we encounter them, notions that close our minds to new and often more accurate information. Remember the Hereditarians we discussed in the introduction to this book? Their preconception that entire ethnic groups and races are mentally deficient profoundly influenced their research studies and wreaked havoc on American education. And all the while they thought they were being scientific!

Be wary of all preconceptions, and be especially alert for ones you may have unwittingly embraced.

Reliance on Feelings and First Impressions

We have noted that feelings tend to be capricious, changing with our moods; deceptive, leading us to regard our wishes as reality; and open to manipulation by those who wish to influence us for their own purposes. We have also noted that the current fashion is to ignore this reality and to trust feelings, hunches, urges, impressions, impulses, and intuitions rather than to subject them to careful analysis. Because this intellectual fashion is arguably the greatest obstacle to effective thinking in our time, it is worth revisiting here.

Feelings may prompt you to do your homework or to neglect it and attend a party, to respect other people or take advantage of them, to be a faithful or an unfaithful spouse, a caring or an abusive parent, to pay your bills or cheat your creditors, to pet the dog or kick it. Interestingly, however, the more completely you trust your feelings, the more astray they are likely to lead you. The first urge is often the least responsible one. For example, you may feel like throwing your trash out the car window, parking in spaces reserved for the handicapped, tearing pages out of library books, and playing your music disturbingly loud. Only when you ask yourself "Is this the right or the best thing to do?" and think about the matter, are you likely to act responsibly. And let's face it, some of the most important tasks are ones we don't feel like doing—practicing the piano, eating nutritious foods, keeping financial records, exercising, and completing unpleasant assignments at work. If we were to do only what we felt like doing, a lot of essential tasks in life wouldn't get done.

Solomon Asch conducted an experiment to learn whether first impressions can preempt thought. Asch asked people to evaluate a person by a series of adjectives. In some cases, he said the person was "intelligent-industrious-impulsive-critical-stubborn-envious"; in others, he reversed the order. When "intelligent" was mentioned first, the participants in the experiment tended to give a positive evaluation; when "envious" was first, they tended to give a negative one.[12] In such cases, as in most everyday situations, the only way to make a reasonable assessment would be to resist the first impression and consider all the adjectives.

The ancient story about the six blind men and the elephant makes a similar point. One of the men touched its side and decided an elephant is like a wall. The second touched its trunk and concluded an elephant is like a snake. The third, its tail—a rope; the fourth, its ear—a fan; the fifth, its leg—a tree; the last, its tusk—a spear. All were firm in their opinions, yet no one had an accurate understanding of the animal. The problem lay not in their lack of sight but in their unthinking acceptance of their first impressions. If any one of the men had walked around the animal and touched each part, he would have formed a more accurate image.

About 2,500 years ago, the Chinese philosopher Mencius noted that feelings are a valuable aid to successful living. He wrote:

> The feeling of compassion is the beginning of benevolence; the feeling of shame and self-reproach, the beginning of righteousness; the feeling of courtesy and modesty, the beginning of propriety; the feeling of right and wrong, the beginning of wisdom. These four beginnings are like the four limbs of man and to deny oneself any of these potentialities is to cripple oneself.

But he also warned of the need to subject feelings to evaluation. "When our senses are exercised without thought and are thereby obscured by material things, we are led astray. Heaven gave us mind and senses. Guided by thought, let us use our senses in the right way."[13]

Mencius's balanced view anticipated and exposed the error of Rousseau and the Romantics, as well as today's fashionable reliance on feelings. Try to remember it whenever you are tempted to follow your feelings uncritically.

ATTITUDES THAT OBSTRUCT THOUGHT

William James, the late nineteenth-century psychologist and philosopher, once remarked: "The greatest discovery of my generation is that a human being can alter his life by altering his attitude." Unfortunately, in the passage of time between his era and ours, that insight got lost. Today, many people have the mistaken notion that attitudes never need altering because there's no such thing as a bad attitude. In reality, any attitude that causes us physical, emotional, or intellectual harm is properly called "bad." Our discussion focuses on the attitudes that prevent us from using our minds effectively.

"I Already Know Everything Worth Knowing"

A lot of people have this attitude. That's why when people are stopped on the street and are asked to name the secretary of state or the approximate geographical location of Iraq, many of them haven't a clue. It's also why many people are content with a very rough approximation of the facts, as the following passages from student writing illustrate.[14]

- A virtuoso is a musician with real high morals.
- H_2O is hot water, and CO_2 is cold water.

- Ancient Egypt was inhabited by mummies, and they all wrote in hydraulics. They lived in the Sarah Dessert and traveled by Camelot.
- Jacob, son of Isaac, stole his brother's birthmark.
- The first thing they do when a baby is born is to cut its biblical cord. [This may explain the previous line.]
- Life begins at contraception.

What makes people develop the attitude that they are already as knowledgeable as they need to be? Probably a combination of laziness, self-deception, and the desire to maintain a good self-image. The problem is that this attitude prevents them from learning. The ancient Greek philosopher Epictetus wrote, "What is the first business of one who practices philosophy? To get rid of self-conceit. *For it is impossible for anyone to begin to learn that which he thinks he already knows*" (emphasis added).

If you have the attitude that you know everything worth knowing, replace it with the following one recommended by one of the most prolific inventors of all time, Thomas Edison: "[I] don't know one-millionth of one per cent about anything." It will open your mind to new knowledge.

"To Challenge My Ideas Is to Disrespect Me"

This attitude is caused by the confusion of people and ideas. You and I and everyone else are worthy of respect because we are human beings. Many great documents affirm this. For example, the U.S. Declaration of Independence includes these memorable words, "We hold these truths to be self-evident, that all men are created equal, that they are endowed by their Creator with certain unalienable rights." But nowhere is it written that all *ideas* are created equal, or that they have the right to be respected. Ideas may be logical or illogical, wise or foolish, helpful or harmful; it is up to people to separate the good from the bad, and the better from the good.

Thus, if someone finds one of your ideas to be flawed, he or she is acting responsibly in challenging it, as long as the challenge is presented politely and tactfully. This is not to say you should be entirely pleased—disappointment is perfectly natural on such occasions—but only that you should not regard the challenge as a sign of disrespect and take offense. A good part of "learning from experience" consists of profiting from criticism.

To improve your attitude toward challenges to your ideas, remind yourself from time to time that every challenge is an opportunity for you to deepen your understanding and grow in wisdom.

"Some Subjects Are Interesting, Others Are Boring"

People with this attitude usually have most subjects neatly categorized. For example, they may regard psychology, sports, and popular music as interesting, and science, economics, and history as boring. In reality, however, there are no interesting or boring subjects, only *interested or bored people*.[c] Moreover, one of the biggest causes of feeling bored is having prejudged the subject as boring!

A more realistic attitude is "Any subject will be interesting to me if I give it the opportunity to engage my mind." This attitude may take a little effort to develop, but the payoff in knowledge and enjoyment will more than compensate you throughout life. People who have acquired this attitude have become fascinated with previously hated subjects, cultivated new hobbies, and mastered new skills, even in retirement years. In the process, their minds have remained vibrant long after others' have atrophied.

"Rules and Procedures Don't Apply to Me"

We live in a world of rules and procedures. Every sport has dozens of rules. There are also rules for driving a car (obey the speed limit, signal before turning), rules for checking out in the supermarket (no more than ten items, cash only), library rules (quiet, please; return books to cart, not to shelves), and rules for video rental (due back Friday, rewind tape). Procedures are equally numerous and cover activities ranging from applying for a job to buying a house or traveling on an airline.

It is fashionable in our culture to consider rules and procedures burdensome. As we noted earlier, advertisers know this and often appeal to our feelings to sell their products; for example, consider the slogans "No rules, just right," "Have it your way," and "On planet Reebok there are no rules." Despite this fashion, many of us follow the rules and procedures, though we may occasionally yield to the temptation to board the plane before our row number is called and we zealously guard our right to grumble.

However, many people have the attitude that rules and procedures don't apply to them. Some are so opposed to being told what to do that they refuse to follow even the suggestions offered in books like this one—that is, strategies that will help them use their minds more effectively. "Thanks, but no thanks" is their motto. "I've got my own way of doing things." They gen-

---

[c] There are, of course, interesting and boring *treatments* or *presentations* of a subject, but that is a different matter that should not be confused with the one being discussed.

erally waste a lot of time and energy, alienate a lot of people, and get significantly poorer results from their efforts than if they followed good advice.

A much more sensible attitude is "Because rules and procedures generally eliminate confusion and increase my own and other people's safety and efficiency, I will follow them unless I have compelling reason not to."[d]

BECOMING YOUR OWN CRITIC

The only really effective way to overcome the habits and attitudes that obstruct thinking is to become your own critic. This entails monitoring what you think, say, and do. No special strategy is required. Just be as observant of yourself as you are of other people. Use your time of daily reflection to review your observations and, where appropriate, identify lapses and renew your resolve.

Given the warnings against self-criticism in the literature of popular psychology, you may be concerned about becoming your own critic. Admittedly, some people are excessively critical of themselves already and for those people to become more so would be foolish and even dangerous. But few self-improvement books make any mention of the opposite extreme—reserving all one's criticism for other people and ignoring or explaining away one's own mistakes. That extreme has harmful effects too, not least of which is the failure to learn from one's mistakes and the increased likelihood of being victimized by them.

Which extreme is more prevalent today? And which extreme are you closer to? The answers to both questions can be found by a long and honest look at your experience.

---

[d] Not all advice is good advice, of course, nor are all rules and procedures reasonable, so there may be times, however few, when prudence or honor requires that they be challenged.

3

RESISTING MANIPULATION

> Most people are other people. Their thoughts are someone else's opinions, their lives a mimicry, their passions a quotation.
>
> —Oscar Wilde

It is not pleasant to think of ourselves as influenced by other people and by the circumstances of our lives. Our desire to be individuals, our "own persons," makes us resist that admission, but such influences are too great to be denied. When we were infants and toddlers and our parents prompted us to say "mama" and "dada," we didn't say "arf" and "meow." We imitated their sounds. If they spoke to us in English, we didn't respond in Chinese or Farsi. When they introduced us to basketball and football, we didn't plead to watch a badminton or cricket match instead. Similarly, we followed their guidance in walking, using a spoon, blowing our nose, and brushing our teeth.

Many of our *ideas* are borrowed from other people, as well. The process begins in infancy and continues throughout our lives. All day long, every day of our lives, we encounter other people's ideas in school, at work, in our neighborhood, and on radio and television. Some of those ideas we soon forget but others take up residence in our mind.

MAJOR CONTEMPORARY INFLUENCES

As recently as sixty or seventy years ago, the chief influences on people were family, teachers, and religious leaders. Today, the influence of mass culture is, for many people, greater than all three of those influences combined; the values and themes of mass culture are presented more visually and/or dramatically and through many more vehicles, including radio, television, movies, popular music, and the Internet. To appreciate the power of mass culture, consider what has happened with the concept of self-love. For many centuries, the consensus of home, school, and church was that self-love leads to narcissism and should be avoided. (My grandfather made the point more bluntly: "Self-love stinks!")

Then forty or so years ago, as the "Age of Me" was dawning, someone decided that self-love is essential for emotional health and said so in print. Other writers adopted the theme and were interviewed on talk shows. Before long, the idea appeared in soap opera dialogue, situation comedy banter, and song lyrics. Soon it became a standard theme in dramatic shows ranging from Westerns and cop shows to stories of the inner city. As for the Internet, I just did a quick search for "self-love" and got 3,780,000 hits, and it's a good bet that the vast majority of those references sing its praises. Such is the power of mass culture—it leads us to accept unquestioningly a lot of ideas that should be carefully examined.

The benefits of the electronic age no doubt outweigh its harmful effects. Those benefits include new opportunities for learning, for communicating with others, and for enjoyment. On the other hand, however, the same age has created new and more effective ways for others to manipulate us. This chapter identifies the various forms of manipulation and presents a strategy for resisting their influence.

Manipulation is defined as using other people for one's own advantage and, by implication, against their own interests. It is characterized by shrewdness and often by deceit. In the realm of ideas, which is our main concern, manipulation commonly involves withholding or falsifying important information or appealing to our emotions in ways that prevent us from thinking. Examples of manipulation can be found in every mode of communication and entertainment. However, we will limit our consideration to the most influential ones: advertising, television and movies, journalism, and political discourse.

Advertising

Advertisers spend billions of dollars a year on print ads and commercials and, in most cases, don't just present the product and explain how it works.

Rather, they prey on our emotions by associating the product with our hopes, dreams, and desires—notably youth, sexual pleasure, success, love, security, and acceptance.

The focus on emotion began in the early 1900s when Walter Dill Scott argued for the use of suggestion rather than reason in advertising. Next, John Watson, the "father of behaviorism," contributed the idea of the "conditioned emotional response," an extension of Pavlov's manipulation of dog's responses to stimuli.[1] Watson rejected the idea of a mind or soul in human beings, regarding them as essentially no different from animals. Thus he believed that buying is an emotional rather than rational exercise and saw the task of advertising as the manipulation of people's emotions.[2] Since Watson's time, advertising has aimed, in the words of a famous expression, at "selling the sizzle rather than the steak."

Today's ads are more sophisticated than those of a century ago, but the essential approach is the same. Every desire, need, urge, temptation, or predilection is fair game for a marketing strategy. Mazda's "It just feels right" and Red Wolf beer's "Follow your instincts" reinforce impulsiveness. Burger King's "Have it your way" promises independence. With many similar products crowding the modern market, there is more reason than ever to use such appeals. As the independent research organization Consumer Reports explains, "Since there's little difference between Coke and Pepsi, the soft-drink giants must appeal more to consumers' emotions than to their reason."[3]

It would be a mistake to consider every emotional appeal in advertising dishonest. The scenes of starving children in tattered clothing used in ads for Save the Children and Christian Children's Fund are designed to produce compassion, but such scenes are genuine and their connection to the message is not contrived but logical. In other words, they reinforce reasoning rather than substitute for it.

Television and Movies

Manipulation in television and movies has occurred for a different reason than in advertising—because of the battle for ratings (or, in the case of movies, box office success). The challenge has always been to keep the audience from shifting to another channel, and in the 1950s and 1960s, when there were only a few channels, the challenge was easily met. However, when competition increased, more manipulative devices began to be used. Of the many events in this evolution, the following are especially noteworthy:

- In the late 1960s, the Children's Television Workshop, best known for the program *Sesame Street*, was founded. According to Jerry Mander,

Sesame Street "was conceived, designed, and executed from its inception by ex-advertising people" and uses many of the same attention-maintaining devices found in ads. Those devices include "a zoom, a superimposition, a voice-over, [and] the appearance of words on the screen."[4] The most basic device, of course, is to change screen images more frequently. Adult programs soon borrowed this device and, over the years, the number of image-shifts has multiplied.

- In 1971, *The French Connection* appeared in movie theaters. One of the most memorable scenes in the film featured the hero driving a car at breakneck speed in an attempt to keep pace with an elevated train carrying the man who had tried to kill him. The image on the screen shifted back and forth from the harrowing bumper-car action on the street to the drama unfolding in the (also speeding) train, as the killer wreaked mayhem on the passengers. The "chase scene" was born.

- In 1981, a new television "cop" series, *Hill Street Blues*, introduced a number of devices that manipulated viewers' focus in order to maintain their attention. The devices included increasing the number of characters appearing regularly on the show from the then-standard few to more than a dozen; making the station house atmosphere more "realistic" by building in extraneous noise and commotion; extending an episode over two or more programs; and, perhaps most significantly, increasing the number of plots from one or two to as many as six or eight and shifting back and forth among them.

These devices quickly became standard in the television and film industries, but they created a problem as great as the one they were designed to solve. By artificially shortening the audience's attention span, they made it more difficult to keep the audience interested. The industries responded with more car chases, fires, earthquakes, hurricanes, and lots of explosions. Murders became more bizarre, close-ups of gore more frequent; eventually, cannibalism was introduced. Sex was similarly used to maintain audience attention, with the same progression to more frequent and more shocking depictions.[a]

Advertisers responded to the decline of the viewing public's attention span by shortening their commercials and adding more attention shifts. The TV industry cooperated because they could sell more commercial

---

[a] The worst invention in history, from the TV industry's perspective, has been the TV remote control, which allows viewer's to manipulate *their own* attention, putting further pressure on programmers to maintain interest.

"slots" and increase their income. Over the past fifty years, the length of commercials has gone from one minute to thirty seconds and then to fifteen seconds.

The attention shifts forced upon today's viewer number well above one per second during commercials and one every few seconds during the TV programs themselves. The total number of attention shifts per hour typically exceeds 800. A simple stroke tally while watching TV will verify this; just make a stroke on paper each time the image on the screen changes. (Questions to ponder: What are the effects of a shortened attention span in the classroom and in the workplace? Is the rise in attention deficit disorder in any way related to the manipulation of attention span?)

Journalism

The most obvious way in which journalism manipulates us is by employing the devices used in advertising, television, and movies. News has become another form of entertainment. The best examples of this are the "morning shows" that feature an assortment of people sitting in living room furniture and mixing banter with information. A steady flow of guests—most of them selling a book, a CD, or a film—ensures that no topic will be addressed for long, lest the audience become bored and change channels.

The challenge to journalists has always been to go beneath the surface of events and explore their causes, consequences, and complexity. This goal has become virtually impossible to achieve as the time devoted to news has shrunk and the emphasis has shifted to superficiality and sensationalism. Increasingly, stories are selected not so much for their importance as for their ability to hold attention—"If it bleeds, it leads."

Even news analysis shows, originally designed to deepen understanding of complex issues, have succumbed to superficiality and sensationalism. It is common these days for guests to be encouraged to comment on matters completely outside their competency. For example, a popular astronomer was frequently asked to give his view on ethical issues, and physicists and biologists are asked about their views on religion. Even more egregious is the common practice of seeking insights from actors on complex matters they know little or nothing about. A talk-show host once asked an actor, "How big a factor in human life do you believe is chance in the universe?" Another host asked an actress, "Did your role in that television drama give you any insights into adoption fraud?" This is like asking someone who played an auto mechanic how to fix a carburetor or someone who played a physician to discuss a surgical procedure.

On many analysis shows, the guests are not experts at all but professional pundits with little or no expertise. As pundit Margaret Carlson explains, "They're not looking for the most learned person; they're looking for the person who can sound learned without confusing the matter with too much knowledge."[b] In addition, guests with balanced or moderate views are told to take more extreme positions. Paul Magnusson says he once received this instruction from a host: "If I ask you whether the budget deficit is a good thing or a bad thing, you should not say, 'Well, it stimulates the economy but it passes on a burden.' You should say, 'It's a great idea!' Or 'It's a terrible idea!' *It doesn't matter which*"[5] (emphasis added).

Even when the hosts genuinely want to probe issues deeply, the demand for a rapid pace may prevent them from doing so. Shows are typically broken into a number of segments, each preceded *and often ended* by a "teaser" for what is to come later in the show. This format reduces the amount of time available for the segments themselves. As much as a third of the entire show is often spent on these "teasers" and commercial breaks, leaving less time for the analysis of issues. It is not unusual for guests to have only enough time to exchange sound bites, and nervous hosts can reduce this still further by interrupting to say "Get to the point" or "You're not answering the question." If time is really short, they may shout over the speaker what they believe he or she *ought* to be saying.

Serious journalists are concerned about these developments. Some years ago, the Committee of Concerned Journalists, many of them well known and highly respected, issued the following statement: "Many journalists feel a sense of lost purpose. There is even doubt about the meaning of [the concept of] news, doubt evident when serious journalistic organizations drift toward opinion, infotainment, and sensation out of balance with the news."[6]

Another way in which modern journalists manipulate the public is by passing off their opinions as facts. Traditionally, facts went in news reports and opinions were confined to the editorial page. Over the years the standard has changed. Today much of the news consists of the journalists' opinions bolstered by quotes from people who agree with them. As award-winning journalist Bernard Goldberg notes, "a reporter can find an expert to say anything the reporter wants—anything!" The trick, he explains, is for

---

[b] Ironically, pundits who appear regularly on talk shows are often given preference over experts when they submit book ideas to publishers. It is not uncommon for book publishers to reject experts' book proposals for no other reason than that the experts are not well known to the general public.

the reporter to call expert after expert until one says what the reporter wants to hear, and then to interview that person.[7] When this happens, the public are manipulated into thinking what the reporter wants them to think.

Political Discourse

Politicians have always been adept at persuasion, but today's media-savvy politicians have brought that skill to a higher and more manipulative level. The chief new tool is the "focus group," which enables politicians to find out where people in general or a particular target group stands on an issue. When focus group activities are highly refined, they can reveal not just the favored position but also the specific words and phrases that elicit the most favorable response—for example, "trust," "family," and "values."[8]

Once the politicians know what the public wants to hear, they can have their speechwriters compose speeches that say it, whether or not they believe it. Moreover, they can use precisely the words they know will be well received, whether or not those words accurately reflect their thoughts. They can also use the magic words in campaign slogans and in sound bites to be used in interviews. When they have won election, they can continue to take their professed stand on the issue and vote accordingly. Or they can take an entirely different position in the hope that the public will have forgotten what they said previously. If, by chance, the public has not forgotten, the politicians can assemble another focus group and find out how to explain away their reversal.

It could be argued that use of focus groups in the manner described is a legitimate political technique. This argument overlooks the fact that politicians serve their constituents' interests when they develop positions in light of the facts, *irrespective of popular notions.* To pretend to do so and instead merely parrot what constituents think is both dishonest and a public disservice.

NOTABLE DEVICES OF MANIPULATION

So far in this chapter we have noted how the major influences on people in our culture have changed in recent decades. We have also noted that the contemporary influences—advertising, television and movies, journalism, and politics—manipulate us in various ways. Let's now examine more closely the specific devices that are commonly used to manipulate us.

Repetition

The more an idea is heard, the more likely it is to be believed. Repetition has legitimate uses, of course, but propagandists and tyrants use it to spread lies. In the 1920s and 1930s, for example, the Nazis repeated incessantly that the Jews were responsible for Germany's financial and social ills. As a result, many Germans tolerated the mistreatment of their Jewish neighbors. More recently, terrorist leaders have used repetition to convince their followers that America is "the Great Satan" and bears responsibility for the world's problems.

In modern politics, repetition that is used to evade or mislead is known as "spinning." A noteworthy example of it occurred in the months leading up to the impeachment of then-President Bill Clinton. During that time, a cadre of White House spokespeople appeared on radio and television programs to discuss the issue. Their spinning consisted of clinging tenaciously to a single theme, that the entire matter was "just about sex" and did not "rise to the level of an impeachable offense." Polls taken at the time showed that this repetition succeeded in moving public opinion in the desired direction.

To avoid being victimized by repetition, remember that the test of an idea is not how many people hold it or how often it is repeated but whether it is confirmed by the facts.

Bandwagon

This is an old technique that says or implies, "Everyone is taking advantage of this great deal. Don't be left out. Act now. Quantities are limited." No one enjoys being left out, and people have been known to buy goods and services they don't really want or need just to be part of the crowd. They have also been known to accept ideas and programs that are not in their own or society's best interest for the same reason. Whenever you encounter the bandwagon appeal, stop and ask yourself: "Is the offer or idea really worthy or am I just being manipulated?"

Glittering Generality

In this device, the advertiser uses words and phrases to imply excellence and uniqueness but offers few if any specifics. "Amazing new discovery," "stunning breakthrough," and "unheard-of softness" are examples of glittering generality. So is the investment company slogan, "You're not just invested—you're *personally* invested." ("Personally" makes the offer sound good but has no discernible meaning.) To avoid being victimized by glittering generalities, refuse to embrace an idea or take an action until you have seen and evaluated the evidence for and against it.

Empty Comparison

This technique uses words such as "better," "bigger," and "more" (as in "more economical") without completing the comparison. What, for example, does "greater cleaning power" mean? Greater than last year? Greater than the competition? Or just greater than water without soap? Such a statement *seems* to make a serious claim, and yet we can't hold the advertiser responsible for it because of its vagueness. Chevrolet's truck division has used the theme "like a rock" for years, yet the visual scenes that accompany the slogan—traveling over rough terrain and pulling heavy loads—have nothing to do with rocks, which just sit there like the lumps they are. Whenever you encounter comparisons, check to be sure they that are meaningful.

Slogans

Slogans are often designed to make us like a product or an idea without any real reason. Dean Witter's "We measure success one investor at a time" is an attempt to make us place our money in that company without knowing why. United Airlines' slogan, "Fly the friendly skies," associates that airline with friendliness. "AT&T—The Right Choice" links the idea of choosing a telephone company with AT&T, an especially clever idea at a time when many rivals exist. The slogan "Michelin . . . because so much is riding on your tires" is accompanied by pictures of adorable babies, leading viewers to associate that brand of tire with the protection of children. Many slogans reinforce current social attitudes. Nike's "Just do it" and Budweiser's "Why ask why? Try Bud Dry" encourage following one's feelings. Reebok's "On planet Reebok there are no rules" celebrates rejection of authority.

Slogans are not confined to advertising, of course. Attorney Johnnie Cochran's famous slogan "If it [the glove] doesn't fit, you must acquit" was largely responsible for keeping O. J. Simpson out of prison. To avoid being manipulated by slogans, ask whether the suggested association has any substance; or, in the words of another famous slogan, ask "Where's the beef?"

Testimonial

A testimonial is an explicit endorsement for something. Actors, musicians, sports figures, and other well-known people are paid substantial sums of money to appear in commercials, lending their credibility and celebrity status to products. More and more, they are also giving testimonials for political candidates and social causes, such as saving the environment or opposing war. To avoid being manipulated by testimonials, ask: How likely is it that the celebrity is merely reciting words he or she has been paid to recite? What qualifications does the celebrity have to endorse the particular candidate or cause?

Transfer

In transfer, a product is placed next to, or otherwise associated with, something well known, respected, or desired. For example, a candidate for office is photographed next to the flag or the Statue of Liberty, or a sports car is depicted with a beautiful model. A similar aim is present in voice-over commercials, in which a celebrity narrates the commercial but is not present on camera. Other examples of transfer are the "party scenes" in alcohol commercials, in which people are depicted having a wonderful time, and the ridiculous soap ads in which people are moaning ecstatically in the shower. Whenever you encounter transfer, ask how useful or worthwhile the product would be without the familiar voice and/or the accompanying images and sounds.

The foregoing devices of manipulation are used mainly, though not exclusively, in advertising products and services. In contrast, the following ones are used primarily in the promotion of ideas and causes.

Stacking the Deck

This technique uses dishonest tactics to make one's own product or idea appear better than competing ones. In a frozen dinner advertisement, for example, the competitor's brand is shown in black and white; then the advertiser's brand is presented in color, piping hot, with steam rising. Some diet and bodybuilding ads feature before and after pictures. In the former, the person is hunched over, frowning, with stomach muscles relaxed; in the latter, the same person is standing erect, smiling, with stomach muscles tightened.

Biased talk-show hosts often stack the deck in their discussions of controversial issues by choosing more qualified and dynamic guests to represent the viewpoints they favor. If, by chance, the other guests seem to be overcoming the disadvantage, the host will interrupt and make it a "two on one" debate. An even more outrageous form of stacking the deck is for talk-show hosts and program directors to ignore entirely the side of the issue they disagree with.

For example, TV discussions of issues involving affirmative action often feature only proponents such as Jesse Jackson, Al Sharpton, Kweise Mfumi, and Maxine Waters. Viewers are thus led to believe that no respected African Americans hold an opposing view. Yet, in reality, a number of distinguished African Americans oppose affirmative action—Shelby Steele, Ken Hamblin, Thomas Sowell, Alan Keyes, John McWhorter, Robert Woodson, Larry Elder, Walter Williams, Roy Innis, Nigel Innis, and Ward Connerly, to name but a few.

Print media also have been known to ignore positions to which they are unsympathetic. In her ten years as a feminist activist, Tammy Bruce had no difficulty getting her ideas published in the *Los Angeles Times*. Whatever she submitted was accepted. Then she became disturbed at what she perceived to be the unfair treatment of Dr. Laura Schlessinger by many gay activists. So Bruce, who is gay herself, composed a short commentary expressing her concern. The *Times* proceeded to hold it for three weeks. When Bruce called to ask what was happening, she learned that an editor had decided not to publish it, essentially because it was on the "wrong" side of the issue. Bruce then withdrew the article and submitted it to the *New York Times*. The editors there proposed an edited version that turned her support of Dr. Laura into *opposition!* Bruce refused to accept the changes, so the letter was never published.[9]

Whenever you encounter a comparison of products, ask whether the deck is stacked in favor of one. Whenever a controversial issue is being discussed, ask whether one side is being put at a disadvantage or ignored altogether. If you detect deck stacking, research the neglected side carefully before making up your mind.

Selective Reporting of Facts

Some news organizations are in the habit of ignoring (or at least downplaying) facts that are unfavorable to their editorial positions or that cast their advertisers in a negative light. Some years ago, the *Archives of Pediatrics and Adolescent Medicine* published two conflicting reports in the same issue. One report said spanking encourages aggressive and violent behavior. The other report, based on a study of more children over a longer period of time, took the opposite view. Any fair news account would have mentioned both studies, but according to author Larry Elder, CBS, ABC, NBC, and more than a hundred newspapers reported only on the report linking spanking to aggression; not a single network and only fifteen papers reported the other.[10]

The spanking case was not an aberration. One research organization studied CBS, ABC, NBC, and CNN reports on the Brady (gun control) bill and found that stories advocating more gun control outnumbered those opposing more gun control by almost 10 to 1.[11] And after President George W. Bush's first national address, CBS News conducted a poll to determine whether the public accepted his tax plan. The poll revealed that 66 percent approved, yet CBS News never mentioned the poll on their evening newscast but instead ran footage of two on-the-street interviews, both of which took a *negative* view of the president's tax plan.[12]

Chances are you've heard that TV viewing has no effect on people's values or behavior. However, you probably haven't heard that hundreds of studies *contradict that claim* because those studies have been suppressed. According to one, television produces "a heightened and unequal sense of danger and risk in a mean and selfish world." Another concludes "Early television habits are in fact correlated with adult criminality." A review of sixty-seven studies revealed a correlation between viewing TV violence and aggression; a review of 230 separate studies demonstrated a relationship between antisocial behavior and the viewing of violent TV programs.[13]

There's no easy way to avoid being victimized by the selective presentation of facts. Your only safeguards are to choose news sources that make a special effort to be balanced and, whenever possible, to check additional sources, as well.

Demonizing People

This device is used to avoid honest debate and consists of characterizing opposing views and people in negative terms. The more inflammatory the label, the more likely it is to breed, at least among uncritical people, suspicion of the person or group being demonized. Among the common labels used for this purpose are "bigot," "homophobe," "racist," "radical," "alarmist," "partisan," "conspirator," and "extremist." (Not surprisingly, people who use such labels for others define themselves as "mainstream," "moderate," and "nonpartisan.")

Tammy Bruce admits that in the early 1990s, when she was an officer in the National Organization for Women (NOW), she and her staff sent out "information packets" that were designed to condition journalists to call her side "pro-choice" instead of "pro-abortion" and the opponents of abortion "anti-choice" rather than "pro-life," thus demonizing people who opposed abortion.[14] Similarly, Victor Crawford, a longtime lobbyist for the Tobacco Institute, demonized antismoking individuals by calling them "health Nazis" and depicting them as zealots who wanted to take away smokers' rights and impose their own values on others. (His admission came after he himself contracted lung cancer and began to feel remorse for his earlier manipulation of the public.)[15]

Whenever you hear one person use a negative label to describe another person, ask yourself what evidence is offered that the label is accurate and whether the person using the label is unable or unwilling to defend his or her position on the issue honestly.

Rumors and Hoaxes

Rumors and hoaxes are lies created for the purpose of deceiving people and, in some cases, getting them to act in a way that is embarrassing or harmful to themselves or others. These lies are especially plentiful on the Internet because anyone can post anything there. There is no editorial mechanism to screen out falsity. Have you seen the e-mail asking you to boycott Tommy Hilfiger because he disparaged blacks, Hispanics, and Asians on Oprah's show? It's totally false. How about the story supposedly (but not really) written by Paul Harvey about Mel Gibson? The story goes that as a young man, Gibson had his face smashed in by thugs. He became so despondent about his appearance that he contemplated suicide, until a priest took pity on him and found a plastic surgeon who restored his appearance. This story is almost totally false. The only truth in it (too small to be redeeming) is that Gibson once played a similar role in a movie. And how about the warnings about the infected needle stories: on gas pump handles, in movie theater seats, or wielded by muggers? All false, as is the one about Costa Rican bananas containing flesh-eating bacteria.

Whenever you hear what is purported to be the "inside" story about anything or anybody, before accepting it and repeating it to others, check its accuracy.

RESISTING MANIPULATION

The fact that there are many devices by which we can be manipulated, and even more people willing to use those devices, does not mean you must resign yourself to being manipulated. You can learn how to recognize manipulation and resist it. In our discussion of the various manipulative devices, we identified some approaches we can take to avoid being victimized. Let's now combine those and some others into an overall strategy:

Know Your Vulnerabilities

Our vulnerabilities are as different as our personalities and mental habits. If you have an especially strong desire for acceptance, you will likely be more vulnerable to bandwagon than many other people. If you tend to be trusting of others, you may be more susceptible to testimonials, rumors, and hoaxes than others. If you are in the habit of trusting first impressions, you may be more easily victimized by glittering generalities and slogans than most people. By making a careful and honest appraisal of your vulnerability to each of the devices of manipulation, you will be in a better position to guard against all of them.

Corroborate Information

When sensible people are diagnosed with a serious disease, they don't begin a treatment regimen immediately—they first get a second opinion. When sensible investors receive a hot stock tip, they don't rush out and buy the stock—they first verify that the stock is a sound investment. Similarly, when sensible people receive information about an important issue, they check with one or more independent, reliable sources to verify its accuracy. Obviously, you shouldn't attempt to corroborate every piece of information you receive; that would be too time consuming. Do so only with information that would significantly affect your thinking about the issue. And be sure to corroborate even when you know your source to be an honorable, responsible person. After all, even honorable, responsible people can make a mistake or be deceived.

Get Both Sides of the Story

Have you ever heard a debate, been thoroughly convinced by the "pro" side, and then equally or even more convinced by the "con" side? If so, you will understand the wisdom of hearing both sides of an issue before making up your mind. Whenever you encounter a presentation of one side of an issue, or a debate in which one side has been underrepresented, make a special effort to postpone judgment until you have checked out the missing or neglected side. You may find it to be more reasonable than you expected. Even if the first side proves to be more reasonable, you will have ensured that your thinking was not manipulated. Remember this insight from Allan Bloom: "Freedom of the mind requires not only . . . the absence of legal constraints but the presence of alternative thoughts."[16]

Talk Back to the TV

We are most vulnerable to manipulation when our minds are passive, and television viewing tends to be a passive activity. Some people solve this problem by getting rid of the TV set. That option, although not a bad one, is too extreme for most of us. Besides, it is possible to keep your mind active while watching TV. One good way is to talk back to the TV, particularly during commercials. Here are some sample responses:

Situation: A stern old company director in an investment firm commercial says to his employees: "Listen not only to what our investors say, but to what they mean,"
Suggested response: "Are your investors so dumb that they say what they *don't* mean?

Situation: A once-great football player promises "up to twenty minutes [of phone time] for 99 cents, and only 7 cents a minute after that."
Suggested response: "Does this mean if I speak ten minutes or five minutes or one minute the charge is still 99 cents? That's a rip off. And why should I pay 7 cents after twenty minutes when other phone companies charge 5 cents a minute all the time?"

Situation: A smarmy scene appears on the screen while off camera someone sings in a trembling voice, "Cotton—the fabric of our lives."
Suggested response: "Why cotton? Why not wool or polyester?

Situation: For what seems the zillionth time, a pitchman for kitchen knives or a miracle soap shouts from your TV set, "If you call in the next ten minutes, you'll get an even better deal, but you must call by then."
Suggested response: "Is someone watching the clock right now ready to cut the deal off? Will I really miss out if I call fifteen minutes from now?" Just for the fun of it, call the toll-free number twenty minutes later, during another silly commercial, and ask if the deal is still available.

Situation: A car salesman announces "Due to unprecedented demand, we are discounting hundreds of cars in our lot."
Suggested response: "What you're really saying is that there's no demand at all, so you've got to manufacture one."

Situation: A woman in a turban says in a lilting, accented voice, "Call our psychic phone line and find out your future."
Suggested response: "If you really can read the future, why don't you pick the winning lottery number and retire?" (Incidentally, a friend of mine received a telephone call from someone who said, "I'm calling for the psychic advice line. We have your name as a person who'd be interested in our service." Without missing a beat, my friend replied, "If you were really psychic, you'd know I'm not interested.")

Read the Fine Print in Advertisements

In the words of an old saying, "the devil is in the details." The details, of course, tend to be put in small print. (The only reason they are in print at all is because of the law against false advertising.) *Consumer Reports* regularly provides examples of this device. For instance, the store that gives you a choice of their special pretzels—the Jumbo bag or the Economy-Size bag. Only by reading the fine print do you discover that the Jumbo bag weighs fourteen ounces and the smaller bag, sixteen ounces! Or the packet that says "Chicken and Rice Soup" in big letters on the front, but discloses in smaller letters on the back that you have to add both the chicken and the broth.

Lots more examples await you in other print ads, as well as on the bottom of your TV screen. The latter scroll by so fast that the only way you can read them is to tape the ad and play it back frame by frame. You'll learn that one long distance ad that claims 5 cents a minute "any time of the day" says at the bottom in tiny print, "7 P.M. to 7 A.M." Also, that the cellular phone company that prominently advertises a low fee of $10 a month and 10 cents a minute if you sign up for twelve months specifies in the fine print that after three months both prices will double. And then there is the letter from a credit card company that asks you: "Why pay an APR of 17.9%, 18.9% or more, when you can pay a low fixed rate of only 4.99%?" According to the fine print, however, "fixed" means four months. No doubt you can guess what the rate will be after that.

Finally, if you have any thoughts of taking the latest wonder drug for your sinus condition, reading the fine print may make you pause because it often says something like, "You may experience such side effects as constipation, diarrhea, fever, vomiting, abdominal pain, fever, sore throat, and abnormal bleeding."

Continue Using the WISE Approach

Chapter 1 introduced you to the WISE approach—Wonder, Investigate, Speculate, and Evaluate. This approach is not only effective for identifying and addressing everyday problems and issues, it is also an excellent means of detecting manipulation and avoiding victimization. Make using it a habit.

4

TESTING IDEAS

Ideas are to the mind as food is to the body. And the rule governing their
consumption is the same: Examine carefully before swallowing.

Raoul and Elena are discussing the issue of whether the use of cell phones
while driving should be outlawed. Raoul is arguing that it shouldn't. At one
point, he says to Elena, "Consider the facts—research hasn't shown any correlation between cell phone use and traffic accidents. The only so-called evidence that has ever been presented for banning cell phones while driving
is speculation. People assume that talking on the phone is a distraction, so
they jump to the conclusion that it's a dangerous practice."

Elena responds, "Sorry, Raoul, but your facts are wrong." She continues her
point, but we've heard enough for our purposes. Her statement is not new. No
doubt you've heard it many times before and may even have said it yourself. Yet
have you ever considered how strange it is? Facts are realities. Saying facts are
wrong seems no different from saying down is up, left is right, round is square.

This certainly sounds confusing. But it becomes clear the moment we realize that the same word can have two or more meanings.

FACTS VERSUS STATEMENTS OF FACT

The word *fact* can refer to reality itself, which can never be wrong; it can
also refer to *statements about reality*, which can be wrong. The expression

"your facts are wrong" means "what you are presenting as facts are not facts" or simply "you are mistaken."

Most false statements are caused by ignorance, thinking we know when we really don't. Suppose someone said, "In the original story, Cinderella's slipper was made of glass." Like most people, you'd probably consider that statement true and feel confident you are correct. Yet the statement is actually false. The original Cinderella story was in French and the slipper was made of fur. The French word for fur sounds like glass and the original translator apparently confused the two.

In some cases, ignorance infects entire cultures. For centuries, almost everyone believed that the Earth is flat and the sun revolves around it; also that whales are fish, mice are spontaneously generated from nonliving matter, and a fever is best treated by letting leeches suck the patient's blood. We laugh at such "facts," but we should realize that future generations will no doubt laugh at some ideas we consider factual.

Not all false statements are caused by ignorance. Some are intended to deceive people—for example, teenagers' lies to their parents about smoking and drinking, and job applicants' inflated claims of education and job experience. The effects of deliberate falsehoods can be far reaching, as the case of Nathan Hale illustrates. Hale became an American Revolutionary War hero after being hanged by the British. Generations of historians reported that his last words before being hanged were, "My only regret is that I have but one life to give for my country." Then research revealed that he never said those words; his biographer merely read the words in a British play and decided to attribute them to Hale. (Some books still contain the error.)

TWO KINDS OF OPINION

The word *opinion*, like the word *fact*, has two different meanings. One is personal preference or taste. This kind of opinion is highly personal. Claude is attracted to petite blondes; Edgar, to tall brunettes. Mary loves the color yellow; Sally, blue. Juwan dresses conservatively; Florence favors wild patterns. Of course, it is impossible to demonstrate that petite blondes are more attractive than tall brunettes or that blue is a superior color to yellow or that Juwan's choices are better than Florence's. That is why the ancient Romans concluded, "There's no sense arguing about matters of taste." That's still good advice.

The other kind of opinion, the one that we are concerned with, is a point of view about a disputed issue. Throughout most of recorded history, this kind of opinion was held in low regard. The ancient Greek philosopher Epictetus argued that one foundation of philosophical thinking is "a condemnation of mere opinion." Nineteenth-century British author Sir Robert Peel termed public opinion "a compound of folly, weakness, prejudice, wrong feeling, right feeling, obstinacy, and newspaper paragraphs." And American author John Erskine sarcastically termed opinion "that exercise of the human will which helps us to make a decision without information."

Since the mid-twentieth century, a different perspective on opinion has become popular. According to that interpretation, everyone not only has a right to his or her opinion but *everyone's opinion is right*, at least for him or her.[a] People who embrace this notion regard their opinions as facts and therefore feel no need to support them with evidence. When others question their opinions, they take offense.

Unfortunately, public opinion polls have dignified this interpretation by lumping together informed and uninformed, logical and fallacious, plausible and implausible, profound and shallow opinions. Some time ago, for example, a roving reporter took his tape recorder into the street and asked passersby "How serious is racial tension in New York?" Among those who responded were a porter, two teachers, a truck driver, a film editor, a security guard, and a secretary. It is a good bet that at least some of these individuals had little or no basis for answering. Yet the reporter never asked about the extent of their knowledge; he just treated all their answers as equal.

Don't be misled by the fashionable view. Having a right to an opinion doesn't guarantee that your opinions will be reasonable, any more than the right to add up a column of figures for yourself guarantees that your answer will be correct. Accordingly, when others ask you to support your opinions with evidence or to explain the thought process by which you arrived at the opinions, don't take offense. They are trying to decide how sensible your opinions are, and that's an intelligent thing to do.

THE VALUE OF EXPERT OPINION

Would you ask your grocer to diagnose a medical condition? When your car quits running, do you call a plumber? Would you pay a shepherd to do your income tax return? No, no, and no. In any such case, you would seek the opinion of a qualified person, an expert.

---

[a] We debunked a related idea in chapter 1, the relativistic idea that each person has his or her own view of truth that is "true for that person."

Are experts ever wrong? Of course. When one psychiatrist says a criminal defendant is sane and a colleague says he is insane, one *must* be wrong. The same is true when one scientist affirms the idea of global warming and another denounces it. The error may not be immediately evident but the passing of time will usually reveal it. Here are some notable examples.[1]

- In 1848, the great American statesman Daniel Webster offered this opinion on the U.S. acquisition of the California and New Mexico territories: "They are not worth a dollar."
- In 1916, a military expert said about the newly invented tank: "The idea that cavalry will be replaced by these iron coaches is absurd."
- In 1932, Albert Einstein (yes, *that* Albert Einstein) offered this expert opinion: "There is not the slightest indication that [nuclear] energy will ever be obtainable."
- In 1945, an admiral advised then-President Harry Truman: "The [atomic] bomb will never go off, and I speak as an expert in explosives."
- In the early days of television, Darryl F. Zanuck, head of Twentieth Century Fox predicted, "People will soon get tired of staring at a plywood box every night."
- In 1957, Prentice-Hall's business editor gave the following reason for rejecting a book on computers: "I can assure you that data processing is a fad and won't last out the year."

If experts can be so wrong, why is expert opinion so valuable? Because more often than not, experts are right. The odds favor expert opinion by a wide margin. Given all this, the most sensible approach is to value the opinion of experts but never to surrender your mind to *a single expert*.[b] Instead, compare the opinions of two or more, at least in important matters.

So far we have seen that something stated as a fact may or may not be a fact and that statements of opinion may be correct or incorrect. This understanding confirms the importance of testing both kinds of statements. We'll consider each in turn.

TESTING STATEMENTS OF FACT

If you were to test every statement of fact you encountered, you'd spend an inordinate amount of time in the library only to find that many, perhaps

---

[b] In this regard, another caution is in order: be wary of experts when they stray from their areas of expertise or make predictions about future events.

most, of the statements in question were factual. Fortunately, there is a more efficient way to work: to test statements of fact only in the following circumstances:

The fact is unfamiliar to you and the original source of the information is unclear. For example, if a friend tells you she just found out an important meeting has been postponed but is vague about where the information came from, it would be wise to check with the person who scheduled the meeting.

You have reason to believe the source of the information is unreliable. A statement of fact made by an author who is unknown or not well respected is more open to question than one made by a well-known and respected author. Similarly, a statement of fact in a supermarket tabloid is more open to question than one made in a highly regarded newspaper or magazine. Prudence demands that statements from questionable sources be verified in sources known to be reliable.

Your own experience challenges the statement of fact. Suppose you are reading a popular self-help book and encounter this statement, "Feelings of guilt are always unhealthy." And suppose that your own feelings of guilt over treating others badly have helped you become kinder and more caring. The opposition between what you have read and what you have experienced would suggest that you check other sources—for example, a scholarly treatment of psychology or ethics—to determine how accurate the statement is.

In the course of testing what seems to be a statement of fact, you may find that it is better classified as an opinion. (It is not uncommon for authors to regard their opinions as facts and to present them as such.) That is the case with the statement about guilt feelings. Though self-help authors tend to regard such feelings as unhealthy, many psychological researchers and ethicists take a more balanced view of them, as we will see when we discuss ethical judgment in chapter 7.

TESTING OPINIONS

Opinions can be tested in a number of ways, the most useful of which are the following.

Assess the Author's Evidence

The most obvious way to test an opinion is to consider the evidence offered in support of it and decide whether that evidence is sufficient in quantity and quality to overcome all reasonable objections. Among the types of evidence careful thinkers use to form opinions are statistics, the results of scientific experiments, case studies, comparative reviews of pertinent research, and expert opinion. (Chapter 6 discusses evidence in greater depth.)

Authors often use less formal kinds of evidence, such as anecdotes from their personal experience or the experience of other people. There is nothing wrong with this kind of evidence, but the details of an anecdote often get embellished as it passes from person to person. And when dealing with a limited number of anecdotes, prudence requires us to ask how *typical* they are. Note: The most vivid and memorable anecdotes are often untypical.

More often than you might imagine, an author will support a broad opinion with nothing more than another opinion or an irrelevant fact. For example, one columnist expressed the opinion that violence in TV and movies has no effect on viewers because people forget what they have seen by the time they reach the theater parking lot. Another writer expressed the opinion that viewing the act of rape in a movie can't possibly influence the act of rape in real life because rape existed long before the invention of cinema.[2]

A caution is in order here. The fact that an author's evidence for an opinion is weak or nonexistent does not necessarily mean that no better evidence exists. The author may just not be aware of it.

Search for Contrary Evidence

In their eagerness to accumulate evidence that supports their opinion, people sometimes, often quite innocently, miss evidence that challenges that opinion. By finding such overlooked evidence, you can identify weaknesses in the opinion that might otherwise go unnoticed. On the issue of whether TV violence is harmful, for example, over 200 research studies document that viewing violence on TV can lead to antisocial behavior. (See chapter 3.)

Occasionally, the contrary evidence can be found in the author's own later work. For example, early in his career as a psychologist, Abraham Maslow was convinced of the importance of high self-esteem; later, he revised that view. Also, early in his career he tended to deny that people are capable of intentional evil actions, but, later, modified this view significantly.[3]

Consider Relevant Situations

Suppose you are evaluating the opinion that the most satisfying response to rude people is to return their rudeness. To test the idea, you might consider how it would work in various situations such as dealing with a snooty sales clerk, having a neighbor borrow things and not return them, and having your dinner interrupted by pushy telephone solicitors. Then you could decide whether a rude response would be desirable in each situation.

Think of Exceptions

This approach works well when you are examining a generalization. Suppose someone said "Religious people are always trying to impose their beliefs on others." Since no qualifying words are included, this opinion is tantamount to saying "religious people in general" or "religious people without exception." So you would mentally review the religious people you know, personally or through reading, and decide whether the person's description fits them. You will probably find that some of those people (like some nonreligious people), though firm in their beliefs and willing to debate religious issues, do not demand that others share their views. Such people are exceptions to the generalized opinion and therefore demonstrate that it is, at best, an overstatement. The more you use this approach to evaluate other people's opinions, the more sensitive you will be to the danger of overgeneralization in your own opinions.

Consider Implications

As a stone dropped in a pond causes ripples that extend a great distance, ideas can have implications far beyond the specific subject they pertain to. For example, some years ago, a study revealed that about a third of all cases of shyness are attributable to genetic disposition. One implication, far removed from biology, concerns whether it is fair for teachers to grade students for not participating in class discussion if they are genetically indisposed to do so.

Consider Alternative Opinions

Even after you have examined two opposing views of a controversy, keep in mind that your choice may not be limited to one view or the other.[c] For example, some people say the way to ensure a quality education for all students is to give poor parents vouchers so they can choose the schools their

---

[c] Of course, if the two ideas are mutually exclusive, you must choose between them. For example, if someone claims a certain country has nuclear capability and someone else disagrees, one must be right and the other wrong.

children attend. Others argue for increased funding of education. But it is not necessary to choose between these proposed solutions—a case can be made for accepting *both*.

You have the same option in many other issues. An alternative to choosing between "the universe evolved" and "God created the universe" is "God created an evolving universe." When Democrats charge that Republicans are beholden to large corporations and Republicans respond that Democrats are beholden to labor unions, you can say "Maybe both views are correct." And when gun control advocates demand handgun registration and the National Rifle Association counters with "Get criminals off the street instead," your response can be "Let's register guns *and* get criminals off the street."

Consider the Consequences

Actions have consequences, some of which are both unintended and unfortunate. For example, the idea of no-fault divorce was advanced to make it easier and less painful for unhappy couples to dissolve their marriages. Legislators and other supporters of the idea had no intention of leaving spouses—usually mothers—and their children without adequate support, but that turned out to be a consequence for thousands. Also, during the late 1990s, many people who were only a few years away from retirement were encouraged by their brokers to keep all or most of their retirement money in the stock market. That turned out to be a bad idea because the market declined dramatically, reducing many portfolios to a small fraction of their previous worth and causing many people to postpone retirement.

Ideas being considered today, of course, will have no consequences until tomorrow, next month, or ten years from now, so in considering consequences you will often be dealing with possibilities and probabilities rather than certainties. Nevertheless, it is important to be thorough in your analysis and not to ignore the unpleasant possibilities.

Play "Devil's Advocate"

This technique consists of challenging accepted ideas—including ideas you yourself are inclined to accept—and seeing whether a valid case can be made against them. Because generally accepted views seem obviously correct, our natural tendency is not to challenge them. Sometimes, however, they are partly mistaken and occasionally they are completely wrong. For decades, it was generally believed that the most effective way to relieve anger is to "get it out"—that is, to express it in words or actions. Then Carol Tavris played devil's advocate, examined relevant research, and found that the opposite is closer to the truth—expressing anger tends to *intensify* it.[4]

Although this is news to our age, it was understood by the ancients. Almost two thousand years ago, Plutarch wrote: "For he who gives no fuel to fire puts it out, and likewise he who does not in the beginning nurse his wrath and does not puff himself up with anger takes precautions against it and destroys it."[5] This example provides another valuable lesson—old ideas are sometimes more insightful than new ones.

BE PREPARED FOR COMPLEXITY

It would be convenient if statements of fact were always neatly separated from statements of opinion, but that is seldom the case. More often than not, they are mingled, with a single paragraph—or even a single sentence—containing both fact and opinion. What's more, there are no labels to help you decide which is which. You must decide for yourself. Consider this paragraph:

> My friend gets upset if a woman holds a door open for him. He seems to feel his manhood is threatened. I believe holding a door open for someone is not about gender roles. It's simply a matter of courtesy.

Only the first sentence is a statement of fact. All the other sentences are opinions, as the clues make clear. The word "seems" in the second sentence signals that the author is offering an interpretation of the friend's feelings. "I believe" in the third sentence signals an opinion. The final sentence merely elaborates on the third.

Be ready, too, to encounter ideas that are partly reasonable and partly not. For example, a mathematics professor appeared on a talk show some time ago to explain a new approach that he called "constructivist math." He began by saying that if a second grader is asked to add 3 and 4 and answers 8, the teacher should withhold evaluation and ask the student how he or she arrived at that answer. So far, this sounds perfectly reasonable.

Then, however, the host asked, "At what point would you explain to the student that the correct answer is 7?" The professor answered that he would never use the words "correct" or "incorrect." Instead, he would say the student's answer was "viable." The host then asked if the university calculated the professor's salary incorrectly and paid him less than he was entitled to, would he say that the university's figure was wrong? With barely a pause, the professor answered, "No, just viable."[6]

A final note: You are likely to feel much more enthusiastic about applying these tests to other people's ideas than to your own. You may even be tempted not to test your own ideas at all. That is a good temptation to resist. Examining your own ideas critically is the surest way to avoid embarrassment when other people examine them.

5

RECOGNIZING ERRORS
IN REASONING

An important characteristic of a quality mind is the ability to detect flaws in other people's reasoning and to purge them from one's own.

- A man once called the administrative office of his town to suggest that the deer crossing sign be removed from his road because too many deer were being killed there. He apparently thought that deer could read signs!
- An elderly woman robbed a bank at gunpoint, then got on her oversized three-wheel bike parked outside and pedaled furiously down the sidewalk. Police caught her a couple of blocks away. She must have reasoned that her bike was so fast that even a squad car couldn't catch it.
- A used car dealer in a television commercial explained why he welcomed customers with poor credit histories: "I'll co-sign your loan even if you've had a bankruptcy. That's because we take the trouble to handpick and inspect [our] cars before you even see them. . . . We guarantee financing because we only sell quality cars." According to this logic, the condition of the car determines the financial reliability of the buyer.
- For years it has been known that the organisms that infect poultry cannot be seen by the naked eye. Nevertheless, someone in the U.S. Department of Agriculture argued that the wholesomeness of poultry could be ensured by *hiring more inspectors*. Obviously, this person

reasoned that microorganisms put aside their natural shyness when a crowd gathers.

Each of these individuals had a train of thought. Unfortunately, it jumped off the tracks. Although the errors here are obvious, they are not so in all cases. Subtle errors are as numerous and often as costly as obvious ones. Logicians have identified over a hundred ways in which thinking can go wrong, but we will limit our consideration to the most common and serious of them.

UNWARRANTED ASSUMPTION

Assumptions are ideas that are taken for granted rather than "thought out." Accordingly, they are usually implied but not expressed. In fact, we may not even be aware we have embraced them. Some assumptions are warranted (justified). For example, when you head out the door to meet friends at a movie theater, you don't wonder whether your car will start, the movie will be the one advertised, and your friends will honor their commitment. You simply assume all these things. Doing so is natural and appropriate.

Assumptions are unwarranted when they take *too much* for granted. For example, assuming that others will pay your way to an event even though no such arrangement was made, or that other people will accept your political views unquestioningly, or that what you hear from the neighborhood gossip is necessarily true.

The following unwarranted assumptions are among the most common and mischievous:

The assumption that if an idea is in our minds, we must have conceived it and therefore should defend it. Many of the ideas in our minds came from reading, watching TV, or listening to people around us. Because such ideas have taken up residence without invitation, they may be evicted without notice.

The assumption that having reasons proves that we have reasoned logically. Reasons may be borrowed uncritically from others. Even if they have been reasoned out, they may be illogical rather than logical, like the reasons offered in support of slavery and genocide.

The assumption that conviction constitutes proof. Strength of belief and correctness of what is believed are unrelated. It is possible to be passionately committed to an error.

The assumption that familiar ideas are more valid than unfamiliar. Familiarity establishes only that we've encountered an idea before. The question of its validity is an entirely separate matter.

The assumption that if an idea is widely accepted, it must have merit. Many people adopt intellectual fashions as they do clothing fashions— mindlessly. Thus, the number of people who have embraced an idea has no bearing on the quality of the idea.

The assumption that the way things are is the way they must be. The way things are is sometimes the result of accident, miscalculation, or malice. The question, "Could this be improved?" is always worth asking.

The assumption that every event or phenomenon has a single cause. Many events and phenomena have multiple causes. For example, a person may have a nasty disposition not only because his father and grandfather modeled nastiness but also because he has cultivated that disposition and is too stubborn or lazy to reform.

HASTY CONCLUSION

A hasty conclusion is a premature judgment, one that is made before other possible conclusions have been adequately considered. If you can't find your camera, for example, you may leap to the conclusion that someone stole it when you may have simply misplaced it. If someone you know is not smiling, you may decide that she is having marital difficulties when she could, instead, be fearful of an upcoming dental procedure or concerned about a relative's health. If a Democrat speaks against a Republican proposal, or vice versa, you may immediately dismiss her criticism as politically motivated rather than substantive when it may be the latter, or a little of each.

The urge to form hasty conclusions is especially strong when the issue is one we have strong feelings about. Not long ago, a member of a well-known political family appeared on a talk show to argue that gas-guzzling sports utility vehicles (SUVs) are wasteful of energy and harmful to the environment. He spoke confidently and with great passion until the host asked this unexpected question: "When you traveled here to be on the show, did you use a commercial airline or a private jet?" The guest at first tried to dismiss the question as irrelevant but then reluctantly admitted he had flown by private jet. The host then triumphantly pointed out that jets consume a great deal more fuel than SUVs and the guest's view seemed hypocritical.

At this point, viewers who own SUVs were probably tempted to conclude that the guest was a hypocrite and his argument had been demolished. But both conclusions would have been hasty. He may simply be a shallow thinker who never considered that his private jet consumed more fuel and polluted more than dozens of SUVs. And advocacy by foolish people does not necessarily disqualify an idea.

OVERGENERALIZATION

Generalizations are judgments about a class of people, places, or things made after observing individual members of the class. A fair generalization fits most members of the class; an unfair generalization—that is, an *over*generalization—does not. The question is always, how many observations is the generalization based upon? One problem is that this information is seldom available. For example, you've probably never heard anyone say "I have met 304 Italians and the vast majority were emotional and animated" or "I have met 298 Scandinavians and almost all of them were calm and reserved." But you may probably have heard people say "Italians are emotional and animated" or "Scandinavians are calm and reserved." So you were left wondering how many Italians or Norwegians the person actually knew. (Given how easy it is to form generalizations, maybe *none*!)

How, then, can you decide if a statement is an overgeneralization? One way is to consider how much observation is necessary to support the statement. A twelfth-century Moorish thinker declared that "races north of the Pyrenees . . . never reach maturity; they are of great stature and of a white color. But they lack all sharpness of wit and penetration of intellect." It is inconceivable that anyone could have had contact with enough individuals "north of the Pyrenees" to support such a statement, so you would be justified in considering it an overgeneralization.

Another way to tell if a statement is an overgeneralization is to consider its source. This way is far from foolproof, but it will often provide a helpful clue as to the statement's fairness. For example, if a dog encyclopedia says "golden retrievers are friendly, obedient animals and made good pets," you can be reasonably sure the generalization is fair. (To be extra safe, you could check one or two other reliable sources.)

A third way to detect an overgeneralization is to consider the context in which the statement was made. In certain contexts, even statements by experts are suspect. A classic example is psychiatrist Sigmund Freud's idea that religious belief is associated with mental illness. He based this idea on the observations he made in the context of his clinical practice. However, virtually everyone he saw in his practice—whether they were religious or not—had psychiatric problems, so his generalization was unfair. Incidentally, psychologist Margaret Hagen claims that the kind of mistake Freud made is much more common in the mental health field than most people realize. She writes: "Clinicians often generalize from single instances [to whole groups or to people in general]." Moreover, "clinical psychology continues to publish hundreds of such cases each year in professional journals and to use them as teaching materials."[1]

Yet another way to decide whether a generalization is fair is to look for qualifying words or phrases, such as "some," "many," "most," or "at certain times," which signify the author's intention of avoiding overgeneralization. When you see such words, ask whether the author has succeeded. For example, "*Some* pit bull terriers are vicious" requires much less documentation than "*Most* pit bull terriers are vicious." Similarly, "Florida beaches are generally crowded in the winter" is a fair generalization; "Florida beaches are crowded" is not. Keep in mind, though, that a generalization can be fair even if no qualifying words are present, as the statement about golden retrievers illustrates.

OVERSIMPLIFICATION

To simplify is to make a phenomenon less difficult to understand without distorting it. Parents and teachers simplify when they speak to children. Physicians simplify when they explain medical conditions to patients. Engineers, astronomers, accountants, and chemists simplify when they communicate with people untrained in their fields.

To *over*simplify, on the other hand, is to present a false picture of a phenomenon by overlooking or ignoring its complexity. Simply said, oversimplification distorts reality, as the following examples illustrate:

- The slogan often seen on bumper stickers "Guns don't kill people— People kill people" says that guns play no role in killing. The reality is that they do play a role. They are an *instrument* by which an *agent* (a person) kills someone. It is impossible to shoot someone without a gun.
- "Selfishness is no different from selflessness. Both involve the pursuit of happiness by performing acts that bring one pleasure." This claim notes the minor similarity and ignores the major difference—selfish people put their own interests above other people's; selfless people put other people's interests first.

- "We're just giving the viewing public what they want" is a common claim offered by television producers in defense of highly sexualized, violence-filled, or otherwise sensational programming. In reality, the producers not only feed the public's appetite but also stimulate it. The graphic sex and violence and relentless sexual innuendo that are common today would not have been tolerated in the 1960s. (In fact, much milder material drew strong objection then.) Such material has become accepted largely because TV producers have "pushed the envelope" and conditioned the public to accept it.
- A *New York Times* writer once offered an argument in support of the oversimplified thesis, "No one has ever dropped dead from viewing *Natural Born Killers*, or listening to gangster rap records." Columnist George Will required only a single illustrative statement to expose the error and undermine the argument: "No one ever dropped dead reading 'Der Sturmer,' the Nazi anti-Semitic newspaper, but the culture it served caused six million Jews to drop dead."[2]
- French existentialist Jean-Paul Sartre wrote, "Childhood decides." He meant that what happens in childhood determines the kind of person one becomes and nothing can be done to change that destiny. Reality, however, is more complex. Even though the experiences of childhood exert a powerful and often lasting influence, people can and do change.

Among the causes of oversimplification are narrow perspective, mental laziness, and the demand for easy answers. To detect oversimplification, ask whether the reality in question may be more complex than the writer or speaker is representing it to be.

FALSE ANALOGY

An analogy is a comparison between things that are very different in most respects but very similar in one or two. Because analogies have the power to illuminate similarities, they are useful tools of explanation, especially in difficult matters. Unfortunately, too much attention to similarities can obscure differences and lead us into error.

That is just what happened in 1633 to a University of Pisa professor who was addressing the question of whether the Earth moves. He wrote: "Animals, which move, have limbs and muscles; the earth has no limbs and muscles, hence it does not move." In 1932, a British physician got carried away by another animal analogy and proceeded to give this advice concerning diet: "If your eyes are set wide apart you should be a vegetarian, because you inherit the digestive characteristics of bovine or equine ancestry."[3]

A more somber example of false analogy was offered by Soviet Communist leader Lenin. When anyone objected to his use of mass murder to attain political goals, he responded, "It is necessary to break some eggs to make an omelette." This makes perfect sense with eggs but is absurd when applied to human beings.

The key to detecting false analogy is to remind yourself that things that are alike in one respect can differ greatly in others.

FALSE CAUSE

Curiosity about the causes of things—people's behavior, social and economic events, even the universe itself—is one of the finest features of the human mind. When the search for causes goes well, we gain genuine understanding and insight. Alas, the search does not always go well. Consider the case of the Boston woman who, after being fired from her job for incompetence and repeated absence, claimed that "the stress of going to work had itself made it impossible for her to do her job."[4] This is a classic example, albeit a silly one, of the error of false cause.

Logicians call this error "post hoc thinking." The term is an abbreviation of the Latin phrase *post hoc ergo propter hoc*, which is translated "after this, therefore because of this." Examples of this error are abundant. If the economy falters (or thrives) after a new president is elected, he is blamed (or given credit), when the true cause of the change may be someone or something else. When a college student gets a low mark on a test, she may remember that she had a disagreement with the professor the day before she took the test and conclude that the professor lowered her grade as a punishment. If your car won't start or you lose your wallet, you may blame the fact that you recently walked under a ladder, opened an umbrella in the house, or broke a mirror.

Whenever someone asserts that something caused something else, ask whether the closeness of the events in time denotes a cause-and-effect relationship or merely coincidence.

DOUBLE STANDARD

In her analysis of Sigmund Freud's view of the human mind, psychotherapist Marjorie Rosenberg writes, "The act of thinking, distinguished by

Aristotle as a peak of human experience, became in Freudian theory most notable as a neurotic exercise designed to inhibit awareness of instinctual needs. Excluded from this interpretation was, of course, the product of Freud's mind—psychoanalytic theory itself."[5] Freud was committing the error of the double standard: exempting one's own ideas from the same level of scrutiny and judgment one applies to other people's ideas.

The error of the double standard is observable today in some champions of tolerance and diversity, who manage to honor these ideals when others agree with them but quickly forget them when they encounter opposition. Freedom of speech, it seems, applies only to people on their side of issues; others they would censor. Examples of this duality are prominent in the discussion of controversial issues such as affirmative action, abortion, gun control, gay marriage, and environmentalism.

Intellectual honesty demands a single standard of judgment, no less rigorous and probing for those who agree with us than for those who disagree.

FAILURE TO MAKE DISTINCTIONS

To make a distinction is to acknowledge the differences between things. Among the important distinctions to be made when thinking about issues are the following:

The distinction between the person and the idea. Some people think they are evaluating ideas when they are merely judging people. They endorse the ideas of people they admire and reject the ideas of people they dislike. Or even worse, they endorse or reject ideas on the basis of how the person who expresses them looks or sounds. Ideas have no control over who embraces them. They should be judged solely on their own merits.

The distinction between assertion and evidence. Assertion says that something is so; evidence documents that it is so. Put another way, assertion tells; evidence shows. Only by making this distinction can we be sure that a writer or speaker is being careful and responsible and providing adequate support for his or her ideas.

The distinction between familiarity and validity. Because we are more comfortable with familiar things than unfamiliar things, we tend to drop our intellectual guard with ideas we have heard before, yet, as noted earlier, there is no logical reason to believe that familiar ideas are more valid than unfamiliar ones.

EITHER/OR THINKING

Throughout this book, we have noted the importance of considering a variety of alternative ideas before making up our mind about an issue. Either/or thinking does exactly the opposite, arbitrarily limiting the alternatives to two. Moreover, it doesn't even let us consider combining those two but, instead, demands that we choose between them. This error can be very tempting and for that reason has victimized many otherwise good thinkers and corrupted many vital issues. Here are some examples of either/or thinking:

We are inherently good vs. we are inherently evil. This ancient controversy continues. The followers of Rousseau and Carl Rogers are still arguing that human beings are essentially good, at least until they are corrupted by society, and some people are still responding that human beings are inherently corrupt. The passion evident in both camps has made many of the undecided see the issue in either/or terms and overlook the moderate alternative view—that human beings possess both good and evil tendencies.

Nature vs. nurture. Another ancient dispute concerns whether the controlling influence in people's lives is genetic or cultural. Neither side seems willing to concede that both factors are powerful, though in different ways.

Discovering self vs. creating self. One of the controversies that has occupied psychologists for decades is whether the process of personal development involves discovering what is already present or creating something new. The line between the two tends to be sharply drawn. Accordingly, the middle ground—the idea that we discover our potentialities and create our abilities—tends to be neglected.

Punishment vs. rehabilitation. Should the purpose of incarceration be to punish those convicted of crimes or to rehabilitate them? Each side has its adherents. Neither side seems interested in the question, "Why not both?"

Faith vs. good works. Either/or thinking can be found even in religious debate. Since Martin Luther made his famous claim of *sola fide* (Latin shorthand for "only through faith is a person saved"), Christians have been caught up in this controversy.[a] Some continue to see it in either/or terms, despite the fact that the Bible provides ample reason to affirm the importance of both faith and good works. (Anglican scholar C. S. Lewis once observed that the question is like asking which blade of a pair of scissors is the more important.)

The point is not that all controversies can be resolved by compromise—many cannot—but that all possible views should be considered before any one view is embraced.

---

[a] The issue had, of course, been raised long before Luther's time.

STRAW MAN

This error consists of pretending someone has said something she did not say, and then condemning her for having said it. Sometimes the error is caused by a failure to pay attention to other people's words. At other times, it is a deliberate misrepresentation contrived to obtain an advantage in debate or to make the other person appear to be an extremist.

Suppose you are having a discussion about the legitimacy of attacking a country that harbors terrorists. You say, "I believe that attacking is justified on two conditions—the country has been proven, and not merely alleged, to harbor terrorists; and all peaceful means to get the terrorists expelled have failed."

Suppose, too, that the person you are discussing the issue with responds, "So you approve invading nations and killing thousands of innocent people solely on the basis of some vague feeling of danger. That is irresponsible." What he is accusing you of saying bears no resemblance to what you actually said. He is therefore guilty of the error of straw man.

Detecting "straw man" is not difficult when the false representation immediately follows the actual statement. But when the false representation is made days or weeks later and you did not read or hear the original statement, detection requires some effort. Here is your best defense against being duped: Whenever someone denounces something said by another person, withhold judgment until you have determined that the attribution is accurate.

CONTRADICTION

Professor Converse ends his lecture on relativism with these words: "Remember that truth is subjective. Each person creates his or her own truth and no one has any business telling others what is true." The bell rings and the professor goes to his office and puts the final touches on his proposal for increasing campus penalties for plagiarism. On his drive home, a police officer gives him a ticket for ignoring a stop sign. He accepts the ticket but feels unjustly charged and vows to fight the matter in court. On arriving home, he hears his wife chastising their son for teasing his sister. The professor then joins in and offers his son a brief sermon on the importance of respecting others. After dinner, Professor Converse attends a meeting of an international committee for human rights and supports a motion for a protest demonstration at City Hall.

In the course of a few hours, the professor has contradicted himself not once but four times—not in the formal sense of having made two mutually exclusive statements, but in the related sense of behaving in a way that challenges his own professed belief. If he really believes what he said in his lecture, consistency demands that he allow others to have their personal truths about plagiarism, the traffic ticket, respecting others, and human rights.[b]

The professor's mistake is undoubtedly an honest one. He is simply unaware of the implications of his beliefs. In this he has a lot of company, as the following examples of contradiction demonstrate:

- In the Middle Ages, Jews were forbidden to enter any profession but money lending . . . and then stereotyped as being overly concerned about money.
- At many times and in many places, white people prevented black people from getting an education . . . and then blamed them for being uneducated and not valuing education.
- Many Christians say that the Bible should be taken literally and not interpreted . . . and then proceed to tell others the meaning of difficult biblical passages. Some also say that faith is a free gift from God . . . and then disparage those who have not received that gift.
- Some members of the U.S. Senate claim to want fair-minded judges who will consider each case on its merits . . . and then refuse to consider any nominee who won't make an unqualified statement of his or her view on abortion.
- People who reject the concept of free will and argue that human beings have no choice in their behavior thank others for their kindnesses, ask permission to borrow things, forgive people who offend them, and apologize for their own offenses. (If people have no choice in the way they behave, then thanking, asking, forgiving, and apologizing are pointless.)
- TV executives claim that commercials influence people but program content doesn't. Film critic Michael Medved exposed this contradiction, noting that it is an "established principle" in Hollywood that "a two-second glimpse of a box of Tide can help the manufacturer" but "two hours of graphic gore" won't hurt the audience.[6]

---

[b] The solution is not for the professor to stop making judgments about these matters but to realize the error inherent in relativism. The statement "truth is subjective" is an *objective* claim about truth and thus is self-defeating. The same can be said of the statement "nothing can be said to be true or false for all people," which makes a claim about what is true or false for all people *even as it denies the validity of doing so.*

ERRORS CAN MULTIPLY

It would be unfortunate enough if errors occurred singly and separately, yet in many cases one causes another and that one may precipitate several more. For example, an unwarranted assumption can lead to a hasty conclusion, a false analogy can lead to overgeneralization, and either/or thinking can lead to oversimplification.

Be alert for errors not only in other people's thinking but in your own as well. And don't be discouraged when you find yourself committing the same ones again and again. As the poet said, "To err is human." Just correct your errors when they occur and renew your resolve to avoid them in the future.

6

ANALYZING ARGUMENTS

We might as well give up the fiction
That we can argue any view.
For what in me is pure Conviction
Is simple Prejudice in you.

—Phyllis McGinley

McGinley is kidding us, of course, reminding us of our tendency to be believe all our views are sagacious and the other guy's are shallow and perhaps even dishonest. An occasional laugh at our foolishness can help to keep it under control.

Let's begin by identifying the various definitions of the term *argument*. It is commonly used as a synonym for *quarrel*—that is, for a disorderly exchange of viewpoints in which more heat than light is generated. This is not the meaning we will be using in this chapter, however. There are two other common definitions of *argument*, both of which are relevant to our discussion in this chapter, but each in a different way. If I say, "Clara and Constantine had a spirited argument over the drinking age," I am referring to *the exchange of views* that occurred between them. On the other hand, if I say, "Clara offered a powerful argument for a uniform drinking age in all states," I am referring to *the specific line of reasoning* she presented. We will use *argument* mainly in the latter sense. Any variation in reference will be made clear by the context.

Let's expand our definition to make it more complete. An argument is a line of reasoning that proceeds from two or more premises (assertions) to a conclusion. A sound or valid argument is one in which the premises are true and the conclusion follows logically from them. An unsound or invalid argument is one in which one or more premises are false or in which the conclusion does not follow logically.

Sound Argument

Human beings make mistakes.[a]
My husband is a human being.
Therefore, my husband
makes mistakes.

Comment

Both premises are demonstrably true, the first by historical data and the second by observation. The conclusion follows logically: If the husband is a member of a class, all of whom make mistakes, he must make them too.

Unsound Argument

No immigrants understand American values.
Julio is an immigrant.
Therefore, Julio does not understand American values.

Comment

The first sentence goes beyond overgeneralization to absurdity. Therefore, no conclusion about Julio's understanding of American values can be drawn from this line of reasoning.

Unsound Argument

Some Swedes are quarrelsome.
Sven is a Swede.
Therefore, Sven is quarrelsome.

Comment

The problem here is not with either of the premises but with the conclusion. If only some Swedes are quarrelsome, then others must not be. We can't be sure which Sven is, so the conclusion does not follow logically.

Each of the above arguments has two premises and a single conclusion. Moreover, the truth or falsity of the premises is rather obvious. In other

---

[a] Whenever a term is not qualified by a word or phrase such as "some," "many," or "who live in Cleveland," the reference is understood to be to *all* (in this case, all human beings).

words, they say the verbal equivalent of $1 + 1 = 2$ or $2 - 1 = 1$. Not all arguments fit this simple pattern, however; some have hidden premises. Others have more than two premises or premises that are difficult to analyze. We'll consider arguments with hidden premises first and then more complex arguments.

HIDDEN PREMISES

The fact that a premise is unstated does not necessarily invalidate the argument. Nor does it necessarily indicate conscious deception—the person may merely be striving for brevity or making an unconscious assumption. Here are some examples of arguments with hidden premises:

Argument	*Hidden Premise*
Victor Vanquish has been a highly successful businessman, so he will achieve distinction in Congress.	The qualities that produce success in business also produce distinction in public service.
Because prostitution is immoral, it should continue to be classified as a crime.	Everything that is immoral should also be criminal.
Low grades cause students disappointment and embarrassment. Therefore, schools should abolish the practice of giving grades.	Disappointment and embarrassment are in no way beneficial.

Obviously, it is easier to be fooled by an unstated false premise than by a stated one. That is why it is important to identify hidden premises and to evaluate them as you do stated ones. Here is how you would proceed to evaluate the three arguments presented above:

In the case of Victor Vanquish, you would ask: Has he been a highly successful businessman? Exactly what achievements constituted his success? Do the qualities that produce success in business also produce distinction in public service? Are there other, perhaps very different, qualities required for service in Congress that a successful businessman might not possess? If so, does Victor possess them? Finally, do the answers to the previous questions support the conclusion that he is likely to serve with distinction in Congress?

In the case of prostitution, you would ask: Is prostitution immoral? Should everything that is immoral be classified as criminal? Do the answers to the first two questions support the conclusion that prostitution should continue to be classified as a crime? (Note: If you decided that some immoral acts should *not* be classified as criminal, then you would say the conclusion could not logically be drawn. Some other line of reasoning, of course, might yield the same conclusion, but that would have to be established.)

In the case of the effect of low grades, you would ask: Do low grades cause disappointment and embarrassment? If so, how frequent and serious are these effects? Are disappointment and embarrassment in any way beneficial? Is it possible that they create motivation to improve performance and thus pave the way to success? Finally, do your answers to the previous questions support the conclusion that grades should be abolished?

COMPLEX ARGUMENTS

Complex arguments have the same basic structure as simple arguments—some premises (stated or hidden) and a conclusion that, in the author's view, follows logically from them. What makes complex arguments different is that they usually have more premises and at least some of their premises require more documentation. Accordingly, complex arguments contain considerable explanation and evidence and are therefore longer, often running to several thousand words (as in a feature article) or tens of thousands of words (as in a book).

The key to analyzing a complex argument is to recognize the relationships among the premises and the relationship between the premises and the conclusion. Such relationships are always implied and often stated directly. The words used to signal them function like the plus, minus, and equal signs in arithmetic. Expressions such as "and," "also," "in addition," "first," "second," and "moreover" signal the addition of premises or supporting material. "But," "yet," "however," and "on the other hand" signal qualifications or exclusions (subtraction). "Therefore," "so," "as a result," and "for these reasons" signal the argument's conclusion just as the equal sign signals the sum in arithmetic. Headings in an article and chapter titles in a book provide similar clues to an argument's structure.

Before considering a step-by-step procedure for analyzing complex arguments, let's look more closely at the variety of evidence used in arguments.

TYPES OF EVIDENCE

The types of evidence used in arguments range from everyday examples or cases in point to formal scientific studies. The following are the most commonly used types of evidence, presented in more or less random order. Next to each are some appropriate questions to ask about it.

Type of Evidence	*Questions to Ask*
Celebrity testimony is becoming increasingly common today because celebrities enjoy media access often denied to others, including scholars. Unfortunately, many celebrities are willing to offer their opinions even when their knowledge is very limited. Thus celebrity testimony is generally unreliable.	Does this person have any expertise in the subject? What are his or her credentials? What support, if any, is given for the person's assertions?
Undocumented reports, also known as gossip or hearsay, come from a variety of sources, notably conversations with friends and acquaintances—the "grapevine," as it were—and also, increasingly, from e-mails and Internet chat rooms. Such reports can even find their way into news reports as statements by "anonymous sources." This form of evidence is generally unreliable.	Where did the report originate? How can the substance of the report be verified?
Documented reports differ from undocumented ones in	Did the report really come from the source cited? Did the

Type of Evidence	*Questions to Ask*
that the source of the information is mentioned either in the report itself or in a footnote or endnote. Such reports are found in newspapers, magazines, and books, as well as in the broadcast media and on the Internet. They are often reliable.	information originate with that source or was he or she merely citing someone else? If the latter, how accurate was the citation?
Cases in point are examples offered in support of the author's view. They may be drawn from the author's experience or from his or her knowledge of the issue. They may also be real or hypothetical. Real examples are preferred for obvious reasons, but hypothetical ones can be valuable if they are plausible. When dramatically presented, cases in point can be very persuasive, but reliability varies.	Are the real cases verifiable? Are the hypothetical cases plausible? How typical are the cases in point? (Are counterexamples as numerous?)
Eyewitness testimony is commonly considered to be the most reliable kind of evidence. However, that is not always the case. The conditions under which the observation occurred may have been poor. For example, the weather may have been inclement; the event may have occurred rapidly; the observer's emotions or expectations may have compromised his or her	What were the circumstances at the time of the event? Could they have compromised the person's perception? What, if anything, might have happened since the event to alter the persons' memory of it?

Type of Evidence	*Questions to Ask*
perception; and/or the memory may have faded or been distorted in the passage of time between the event and the testimony.	
Expert opinion can be highly reliable but is not always so. It is as difficult to become an expert in a small area of one field today as it was to become an expert in several broad fields a hundred years ago. And, due to the knowledge explosion, keeping abreast of new developments in one's field is even more difficult.	Does the person have expertise in the specific area in question? Do other experts in the field agree, or is this expert's view a minority opinion?
Experiments are of two broad types. Laboratory experiments permit researchers to vary conditions and identify causes and effects with precision. Field experiments have the advantage of occurring in a natural setting. However, the presence of the researchers can subtly influence the outcome of a field experiment. The reliability of either kind of experiment is high, particularly if it has been independently replicated.	Have the findings of the experiment been independently confirmed by other researchers? Have the researcher's peers commented on his or her findings? If so, do they support the findings?
Statistics, in the broad sense, means any quantified data. Statistics are available in virtually every field of knowledge. The reliability of	Is the source of the statistical data reliable? How long ago were the statistics compiled? Have conditions changed since then?

Type of Evidence	*Questions to Ask*
statistics depends on the degree of care exercised in collecting and analyzing data. Gregg Easterbrook's witty observation, "Torture numbers and they'll confess to anything," is grounded in reality.	
Surveys are technically a subdivision of statistics, but they differ from other kinds of statistics in the way their data are typically obtained—by representative sample rather than all members of a group. The sample may be random, systematic (for example, every twentieth name in the telephone book), or stratified (that is, reflecting the proportions of the group). The contacts may be in person, by telephone, or by mail. Surveys are about as reliable as other forms of statistics and for essentially the same reasons.	Was the survey representative of the group studied? Were the questions clear and objectively phrased? If the survey was mailed, what percentage of people failed to respond? Was the number high enough to compromise the study?
Formal observational studies are of two types. In a *participant* study, the observer takes part in the activity being studied—for example, by serving as a member of the crew on a scientific exploration. In a *detached* study, the observer does not participate— for example, the observer would simply watch people's reactions at a neighborhood	Could the outcome of the study have been influenced by the presence of the observer? Was the study of sufficient duration to support the findings?

Type of Evidence	*Questions to Ask*
forum. Information gained from either type of study is often highly reliable.	
Research reviews are usually done only when a considerable number of studies already exist. The reviewer examines all those studies (sometimes totaling in the hundreds), compares their findings, and reports on the agreements and disagreements. More than any other type of evidence, research reviews provide an overview of the state of knowledge of a subject. Their findings therefore tend to be highly reliable.	Were any important studies not covered in the review?

One important question applies to any item of evidence presented in an argument: Is it *relevant* to the issue being discussed? A piece of evidence may be well documented and yet have no bearing on the argument in question.

HOW MUCH EVIDENCE IS ENOUGH?

One challenge that arises in evaluating arguments is deciding whether the evidence offered is sufficient. No formula exists for making this decision. Sometimes a modest amount of informal evidence, such as a fact or two from history, is all that is needed. For example, one psychologist stated that people who are physically and emotionally abused on many occasions are more likely to suffer traumatic amnesia than people who are abused only once or twice. Another psychologist believed the view was mistaken and wondered what evidence would demonstrate this. The answer she came up with was the well-known fact that victims of slavery and the Holocaust, who suffered horrible abuse over a long period of time, never forgot the experience. No more evidence than that was needed.[1]

More ambitious arguments, of course, would require more evidence. Here are some examples of controversies and the kinds of evidence that we might reasonably expect to find in any serious pro or con argument. In each case, the evidence cited is illustrative rather than exhaustive. Depending on the particular assertions made, other types of evidence might also be necessary.

The Controversy	*Appropriate Evidence*
Does home schooling prepare students as well for college as formal classroom education does?	Comparative statistics concerning Scholastic Admissions Test (SAT) scores, percentages of students attending college, grade point averages in college, and percentages graduating from college. Documented reports of advantages and disadvantages of each kind of preparation for college. Testimony of college admissions directors, academic deans, and other educational experts. Cases-in-point.
Is there a liberal bias in modern journalism?	Documented reports of liberal and conservative bias and a determination of the frequency of each. Cases in point that demonstrate bias. Expert opinion—for example, the conclusions of journalists and other scholars who have studied the issue.
Does the judicial system deal more harshly with black and Hispanic perpetrators of crimes than with white perpetrators?	Comparative federal and state statistics concerning length of sentences, dismissal/reduction of charges, plea bargains, early release, and terms of probation. Expert opinion. Research reviews.

ANALYZING COMPLEX ARGUMENTS

Having identified how complex arguments differ from simple ones and examined the most common kinds of evidence found in complex arguments, we can now consider how this understanding can be combined into an effective strategy for analyzing such arguments.

Determine the Argument's Structure

Once you have read the argument carefully enough to be thoroughly acquainted with it, look back over it and identify the main premises and the conclusion.[b] Often, for the sake of clarity, the author will state the conclusion early in the article or book and then restate it for reinforcement at or near the end. In most cases, the author will also use "and," "but," and "therefore" or their equivalents throughout the work to mark the relationships of the ideas.

If, for some reason, these signs are not present or you have trouble finding them, ask yourself these questions: *What is the main idea the author is advancing?* That will be the argument's conclusion. *What reasons is the author offering in support of that main idea?* Those will be the premises.

Check for Hidden Premises

Once you have identified the structure, you should be able to tell whether a premise has been left unstated. If that is the case, put the unstated premise into words.

Summarize the Argument

The longer and more involved the argument, the more difficult it is to analyze. Summarizing will enable you to reduce a long article to a few sentences and an entire book to a long paragraph. An effective article summary consists of just the argument's premises and conclusion. An

---

[b] You can apply this same approach to spoken arguments that have been preserved on tape. Just replay the tape one or more times. To apply this approach to a live, unrecorded presentation is more difficult, of course, but once you have become skilled in using the approach, you should be able to capture the argument's structure and evidence in your notes as the person is speaking.

effective book summary consists of the *primary* premises and the conclusion. (Books also contain numerous *secondary* premises, which you
should omit.)

Ask Appropriate Questions

The simplest way to do this is to turn each of the statements in your
summary—that is, the premises and the conclusion—into a question. This
will help you to resist the error of accepting an idea merely because it is familiar to you. It will also help to focus your inquiry. Your summary, together
with appropriate questions, will usually look something like this:

Sample Summary	*Questions*
The family is the essential	Is the family the essential
element of society. When it is	element of society? Does
weakened, the entire society	society suffer when the family
suffers. Many of the social	is weakened? Can many social
problems we are experiencing	problems be traced to
today can be traced to	dysfunctional and broken
dysfunctional and broken	families? Does any
families. One major cause of	entertainment mock traditional
the breakdown of the family is	values and hold parents up to
entertainment that mocks	ridicule? Do any (many?) books
traditional values related to	and magazines emphasize self
marriage and holds parents up	at the expense of others? Is
to ridicule. Another cause is	there a "cult of celebrity" and
the emphasis in books and	does it create bad role models?
magazines on self-assertion and	Do these "causes" weaken
self-gratification, even at the	the family? Would overcoming
expense of others. A third cause	them strengthen the family?
is the cult of celebrity, which	
turns many irresponsible	
narcissists into role models.	
As long as these causes	
continue to exert their	
influence, the family will	
continue to weaken and our	
social problems will increase.	

Evaluate the Argument

As we noted early in this chapter, an argument is a line of reasoning that proceeds from two (or, in the case of complex arguments, more) premises to a conclusion. *In a sound argument, the premises are true and the conclusion follows logically from them.* At this stage, having determined the argument's structure, identified any hidden premises, summarized the argument, and raised significant questions, you are ready to complete your evaluation:

- First, address each of the questions you raised about your summary. Look back at the article or book and decide whether the author's evidence is sufficient to establish the truth of the premises.
- If the premises prove to be true, decide whether the author's conclusion follows logically from them. Errors can occur at any point in one's thinking. This means that an author can be meticulously accurate in his or her premises and then draw an overgeneralized or oversimplified conclusion. Be alert for this possibility.

One final point must be made, and it is an important one: The fact that a line of reasoning is invalid means only that the conclusion does not follow logically from the premises. It does not mean that the conclusion is necessarily false.

For example, at the beginning of this chapter we examined some simple arguments. One was: *No immigrants understand American values. Julio is an immigrant. Therefore, Julio does not understand American values.* The other was: *Some Swedes are quarrelsome. Sven is a Swede. Therefore, Sven is quarrelsome.* When we judged both those arguments to be unsound, we were not saying the conclusions are false, but only that they cannot be reached by the stated lines of reasoning—Julio might or might not understand American values and Sven might or might not be quarrelsome. Whether or not different lines of reasoning would lead logically to those same conclusions remains an open question.

7

MAKING ETHICAL JUDGMENTS

Morality, like art, consists in drawing the line somewhere.

—Gilbert Keith Chesterton

Historically, two separate disciplines have laid claim to the subject of ethics: religion and philosophy. Religion approaches moral issues from the standpoint of faith—that is, belief that God has provided a standard (for example, the Ten Commandments) for moral living and that ethical judgment consists of applying that standard to particular cases.[a] Philosophy relies on reason to reveal both the standard and its application.

Some people reduce this distinction to the simple formula *religion equals faith, philosophy equals reason*. However, the matter cannot be summed up so neatly. Most religious ethicists consider reason to be an essential complement to faith, and the relatively small number who do not are nevertheless forced to use reason when dealing with issues not specifically addressed in their sacred writings. In addition, all philosophical ethicists have *faith* in the efficacy of reason; otherwise, it would have no value to them. Many philosophers, of course, also have religious faith.[b]

---

[a] Some people make a distinction between *ethical* and *moral* and between *ethics* and *morality*, but it is a distinction without much of a difference. The words have essentially the same meaning and we will use them interchangeably.

[b] In fact, if agnosticism and atheism are properly considered varieties of faith, it is fair to say that *all* philosophers have religious faith.

The most important question is not whether religion or philosophy is a better guide to ethical judgment; rather, it is which approach is most appropriate for ethical discussion and debate among people of *different* religious and/or philosophical perspectives. The answer is the philosophical approach. To say this is not to disparage religion; it is simply to acknowledge the fact that reason can serve as a bridge between different perspectives and faith cannot. Interestingly, in a great many cases, reason reaches conclusions that affirm faith. To cite but one example, the principle of respect for persons is found in both religious and secular ethics.

Accordingly, we will use the philosophical approach in this chapter. In other words, we will observe the same axioms of thinking, employ the same general strategies, and strive to overcome the same obstacles and logical pitfalls discussed in previous chapters. We will, however, use a special set of criteria. Before we discuss those criteria, let us examine an important controversy about ethics.

THE "OUGHT" CONTROVERSY

Scottish philosopher David Hume, a contemporary of Jean-Jacques Rousseau, argued that reason cannot get us from knowing *what is* (factual knowledge) to knowing *what ought to be* (moral rules or principles). Accordingly, he joined Rousseau in concluding that the basis of ethics is feelings rather than thought. This view paved the way for both moral and cultural relativism and was a contributing factor in philosophy's virtual abandonment of ethics and psychology's subsequent takeover of the subject.[c]

Humanistic Psychology, in particular, has looked with disfavor on moral judgment of either people or actions. The ethical system known as Values Clarification embodies this view, the word "values" representing whatever view anyone happens to have embraced, and "clarification" denoting a process in which people exchange viewpoints with the understanding that no viewpoint is superior to another. In Values Clarification, the analysis and debate that have characterized ethics for centuries are considered taboo.

On the face of it, not judging other people's behavior sounds admirably broadminded and democratic, particularly in a freedom-loving age such as

---

[c] Moral relativism is the belief that whatever a person regards as right or wrong *is* right or wrong for that person. Cultural relativism is the belief that whatever is accepted as right or wrong within a culture *is* right or wrong for that culture. Under both systems, analysis and judgment by others is considered unacceptable.

ours. For example, the nonjudgmental view of adultery holds that if a married person chooses to have sex with someone other than his or her spouse, then it is moral for that person to do so, and anyone who objects is being intolerant. Judgments across cultures are similarly proscribed. Accordingly, if an Eskimo host follows the tradition of letting his male guests sleep with his wife, then the custom is moral, and anyone with a proper appreciation of cultural diversity will treat it as such.[d]

Inevitably, the principle of nonjudgmentalism was extended to a wider variety of issues. Today, people also invoke it in cases of pedophilia, genital mutilation, torture, genocide, and terrorism. They say things like, "I would never be a pedophile but I think it is intolerant to condemn those who are" and "Cultures that practice cannibalism have a different value system than ours, but that is not to say ours is better."

Was Hume right in claiming there can be no basis for moral judgment? Are the reduction of ethics to historical narrative and the ascendance of relativism positive developments? Before deciding, we need to consider the objections to Hume's view.

THE CASE FOR "OUGHT"

At least five objections may be raised concerning Hume's view and the relativism that derives from it. Let's examine each of them in turn.

Objection #1

Even people who counsel against using *ought,* and its synonyms *should* and *must,* use those very words themselves. That includes Hume! Consider these examples from his *Enquiry Concerning Human Understanding* (emphasis added in each case):

> . . . Where there is an opposition of arguments, we *ought* to give the preference to such as are founded on the greatest number of past observations. . . .
> . . . Our present philosophers, instead of doubting [a certain historical] fact, *ought* to receive it as certain, and *ought* to search for the causes whence it might be derived. . . .

---

[d] For some odd reason, people who talk that way never seem to consider whether *the aggrieved spouse(s)* in the first case and the wife who is treated like an object in the second have a legitimate basis for objecting.

. . . Whoever can either remove any obstructions [to science and learning], or open up any new prospect, *ought* so far to be esteemed a benefactor to mankind.

Hume also used *ought* in one of his most famous lines, which incidentally reveals his preference for emotion over thought: "Reason is, and *ought* only to be the slave to the passions" (emphasis added). Hume's supporters would point out that none of the statements cited are *moral* prescriptions. That is true, but they are certainly imperatives and therefore first cousins to moral prescriptions. To my knowledge, Hume never explained why *oughts* are appropriate in every intellectual pursuit except ethics.

In our day, people who support the idea that it is impossible to get from *is* to *ought* manage to make exceptions for their pet causes. They tell us, for example, that it is morally wrong to drive gas-guzzling SUVs, spank children, and smoke in public places. The same is true of ethical relativists such as Joseph Fletcher, the popularizer of "situation ethics." In the very same book in which he denounced the use of *never, always*, and similar absolute terms, he made the absolute statements "Love is the only norm" and "No unwanted babies should ever be born."[1] Norman Geisler has pinpointed the quandary that Fletcher and other relativists face: they must either be absolutely sure that there are no absolutes, in which case they are contradicting themselves; or they must be unsure and, therefore, must admit there may be absolutes.[2]

Objection #2

Much of the folk wisdom in all cultures, as well as much of the counsel offered by sages throughout history, tell us what we should or ought to do. An ancient Hindu proverb claims that "He who is asked for alms should always give." The Chinese philosopher Confucius taught his followers that "Likes and dislikes should not affect our judgment. We should be on the side of what is right and against what is wrong." An Arabian proverb advises that "The words of the tongue should have three gatekeepers: Is it true? Is it kind? Is it necessary?" And Aristotle counseled his followers, "To enjoy the things we ought and to hate the things we ought has the greatest bearing on excellence of character."

In addition to being enshrined in folk wisdom, *ought* and *should* are an integral part of the most thoughtful and revered political proclamations of human freedom and dignity. The Declaration of Independence "solemnly publish[es] and declare[s], That these United Colonies are, and of Right *ought* to be free and Independent States; that they are Absolved from all Allegiance to the British Crown, and that all political connection between them and the

State of Great Britain, is and *ought* to be totally dissolved" (emphasis added). The Virginia Declaration of Rights, on which Jefferson patterned his declaration, contains even more *ought* statements, including these (emphasis added):

> That government is, or *ought* to be, instituted for the common benefit, protection, and security of the people, nation or community;
> That elections of members to serve as representatives of the people in assembly *ought* to be free;
> That all power of suspending laws, or the execution of laws, by any authority without consent of the representatives of the people is injurious to their rights and *ought* not to be exercised.
> That excessive bail *ought* not to be required, nor excessive fines imposed; nor cruel and unusual punishments inflicted.

After the Nazi trials for crimes committed against humanity during World War II, the international community created the Nuremberg Code, which forbids experiments on human beings without their explicit consent; it also forbids experiments that expose patients to unnecessary suffering, disabling injury, or risk of death even with their consent. In that 500-word document, the word *should* is used *thirteen times!*

The laws enacted by legislative bodies provide innumerable examples of moral judgments. For example, the laws against theft, discrimination, rape, kidnapping, and murder say, in effect, that those behaviors are wrong and, therefore, ought not and will not be tolerated. (It can hardly be argued that such laws derive from feeling rather than reason.)

Objection #3

All but the smallest agencies, institutions, associations, and corporations have codes of ethics in which they specify the standards that members and employees are expected to meet. The various *ought* statements or their equivalent found in these codes reflect the reasoned judgment of the organization in light of the experience of its members and employees. Here are just a few examples of such statements:

> American Institute of Certified Public Accountants: "A member should maintain objectivity and be free of conflicts of interest in discharging professional responsibilities."
> American Medical Association: "Physicians have an ethical obligation to report impaired, incompetent, and unethical colleagues in accordance with the legal requirements in each state."

American Historical Association: "All historians should be guided by the same principles of conduct . . . should carefully document their findings . . . should acknowledge the receipt of any financial support, sponsorship, or unique privileges (including privileged access to research material) related to their research."

Objection #4

We all make choices on the basis of *oughts* every day of our lives: Will we go to work or call in sick? Follow the research protocol or violate it? Put quotes around borrowed phrasing or pretend the words are our own? Answer a colleague's question truthfully or lie? Stop for the red light or go through it? Pay the bills or spend the money on entertainment instead? Respond to our spouse's need for appreciation and affection or ignore it? Communicate with our children or rebuff them? Pet the cat or kick it? Moreover, if we are responsible people, we follow reason in such cases even if doing so goes against our feelings.

Most people also make judgments on what *other people*, including people in other cultures, ought to do and not do. When an Asian dictator tortures his political opponents, a gunman in Europe sprays automatic gunfire into a post office lobby, a Middle Eastern suicide bomber kills a hundred people in a shopping mall, an African warlord makes sex slaves of little girls as payment for their fathers' debts, even relativists are inclined to set aside their theory and protest. Actions such as these cry out for condemnation regardless of how the perpetrators or anyone else may feel about them or how embedded they are in cultural tradition.

So far we have seen that virtually everyone does what Hume suggested cannot be done—that is, they use reason to make moral judgments and form moral principles. As American philosopher Charles Sanders Peirce noted, "Good morals and good reasoning are closely allied."[3] Moreover, the judgments and principles prove insightful much of the time, suggesting what the fifth objection will confirm, that Hume was mistaken.

Objection #5

There is a way for reason to produce moral judgments and principles— by starting with an *ought* statement that requires no proof but is self-evident. One such statement is "We ought to do good and avoid doing evil." This is self-evident because the definition of good is "that which is positive or desirable" and the definition of evil is "that which is negative or undesir-

able." Another such *ought* statement is "We ought to desire everything really good for us and nothing else."[e] The latter statement, which Mortimer
Adler calls the principle of right desire, is also self-evident because its
opposite—that we ought to want what is bad for us or not want what is good
for us—is inconceivable.[4]

Starting with a self-evident statement provides a standard for evaluating
ethical issues. No matter what the issue, or how many or complex the details, the fundamental question will be, "What action is most consistent with
doing good or avoiding evil?" (Or "What is really good and desirable and
what is not?")

Is it in any way offensive to classify actions as morally good or bad? Of
course not. Biologists distinguish between healthful and harmful bacteria,
normal and defective genes; psychologists speak of self-enhancing and self-
destructive behavior; tax accountants distinguish legitimate from illegiti-
mate deductions. The same process of differentiation is indispensable in
deliberations about the character of human behavior. There was as much
insight as jest in Samuel Johnson's remark about an acquaintance: "If he
does really think that there is no distinction between virtue and vice, why,
sir, when he leaves our houses let us count our spoons."

OBJECTIVE MORALITY

We noted in the introduction that the humanistic psychologist Carl Rogers
popularized subjective morality by claiming "when an activity *feels* as
though it is valuable or worth doing, it *is* worth doing." We also noted that,
though feelings can prompt us to worthy and even noble behavior, they
tend to be capricious. As often as not, they also deceive us and leave us vulnerable to manipulation. In short, a subjective moral standard is too unreliable to be useful. What is needed is an objective standard.

What constitutes an objective standard? Some say the majority view of the
society or culture we live in. However, majorities have been known to be
wrong. At various times and in various places, they have approved human
sacrifice, infanticide, and slavery. Others say conscience, the "still, small
voice" that whispers moral guidance. Unfortunately, that "voice" is easily
suppressed. As Samuel Johnson observed, "We not only do what we approve,
but there is danger lest in time we come to approve what we do, though for

---

[e] Some philosophers would classify this second statement as a variant of the first one.

no other reason than that we do it. A man is always desirous of being at peace with himself; and when he cannot reconcile his passions to [his] conscience, he will attempt to reconcile his conscience to his passions."[5]

Adding to the problem is that certain popular ideas encourage the defective thought process Johnson described. Consider, for example, these statements from prominent promoters of self-esteem: "Everything I do is an attempt to meet legitimate needs" and "It's all right to meet my needs as I see fit."[6] No one who accepts such ideas is likely to pay much attention to his or her conscience, let alone invest the effort to make it reliable.

Consider, too, the view of guilt typically advanced in modern self-help books. One popular author calls guilt "useless" and goes on to say that "guilt is not a natural behavior" and that "guilt zones" should be "exterminated, spray-cleaned and sterilized forever."[7] The problem is that banishing guilt weakens one's conscience. Thomas Sowell compares guilt to physical pain and calls it an alarm system that saves us from danger, adding that though guilt is as unpleasant as pain, it is necessary for personal responsibility.[8] Willard Gaylin, psychiatrist and cofounder of the Hastings Center for the study of ethical issues, shares this view. He claims that "all the pop psychologists are misleading people about guilt and conscience. Guilt is a noble emotion; the person without it is a monster."[9]

Objective morality differs from subjective morality in that it sets aside personal feelings, preferences, and habitual responses. In other words, it seeks an accurate assessment of the moral quality of actions instead of approval for what we have done or would like to do. Objective morality is based on the principle of respect for persons and judges actions according to the criteria that flow from this principle: obligations, ideals, and consequences.

RESPECT FOR PERSONS

This ethical principle, which may be traced to the religious belief that human beings are "created in the image and likeness of God," is found in most ethical systems. It is also central to democratic societies. The U.S. Declaration of Independence, for example, begins with the words, "We hold these truths to be self-evident, that all men are created equal, that they are endowed by their Creator with certain unalienable rights, that among these are Life, Liberty, and the pursuit of Happiness." The idea is that human rights are not bestowed by any government—instead, they are inherent in every person and must be acknowledged and respected by government.

The specific requirements of the principle of respect for persons are:

First, that each and every person should be regarded as worthy of sympathetic consideration, and should be so treated; secondly, that no person should be regarded by another as a mere possession, or used as a mere instrument, or treated as a mere obstacle, to another's satisfaction; and thirdly, that persons are not and ought never to be treated in any undertaking as mere expendables.[10]

CRITERIA FOR ETHICAL JUDGMENT

For the principle of respect for persons to be meaningful in everyday living, we must be able to determine when it is being honored and when it is being violated. In other words, we need specific criteria to use in judging actions. Those criteria are obligations, ethical ideals, and consequences.

Obligations

Obligations arise from our relationships with other people or institutions. The most obvious kinds of obligations are contractual ones, in which we make a formal commitment to do or refrain from doing something. These are not only morally binding but also legally enforceable. Other important kinds of obligations include the following:

- Obligations of friendship entail mutual respect and support and the keeping of confidences.
- Obligations of citizenship include loyalty to one's country and respect for its principles and laws (provided they are just and ethical), as well as the responsibility to join in the country's defense against unjust aggression. In a democracy, participating in the electoral process is also a moral obligation.
- Employment obligations exist for both employee and employer. Employees have the moral duty to perform assignments conscientiously, to be cooperative with their associates, and courteous and helpful to customers and/or clients. Employers are obligated to pay fair wages and to maintain a safe and healthful workplace.
- Professional obligations are assumed when one is admitted to the practice of a profession. Such obligations are usually expressed in the professional association's code of ethics. For example, membership in a

medical association requires making patients' health a paramount concern, and membership in a scholarly association requires one to demonstrate integrity in research and the reporting of findings.

Whoever willingly enters into any of these relationships is required to honor the associated obligations. To fail to do so is to behave unethically.[f]

Ethical Ideals

Ethical ideals are standards of moral excellence. Unlike obligations, such ideals are not linked to specific relationships but apply to situations and/or people in general. To honor an ethical ideal is not to fulfill a requirement but to strive for nobility. The following ideals are found in most cultures:

- Prudence. To be prudent is to choose one's words and actions carefully and thoughtfully rather than impulsively.
- Justice. To be just is to be fair and to give each person his or her due. It is the opposite of favoritism and prejudice.
- Temperance. To be temperate is to avoid the extremes of behavior and to exercise control over one's desires and emotions.
- Courage. In addition to its obvious physical dimension, this ideal also has an intellectual dimension. The latter entails willingness to seek the truth, however unpleasant it may prove to be.
- Loving Kindness. This ethical ideal is perhaps the most universal of all. It is found in every religion from Baha'i to Zoroastrianism, as well as in secular philosophy, and is embodied in the Golden Rule: "Do unto others as you would have them do unto you."
- Integrity. To have integrity is to be honest and truthful in all one's dealings.
- Forgiveness. This ideal consists in granting others absolution for their offenses against us. (In Christianity, forgiving others is a precondition for receiving God's forgiveness for ourselves.)
- Remorse. This ideal is often misunderstood to mean merely feeling sorry for our offenses. However, it also entails expressing that sorrow in an apology to the one offended and, where possible, making reparation—that is, undoing the harm we have done.

---

[f] An "obligation" that entailed committing a moral or legal offense would, of course, not be binding.

- Gratitude. To have gratitude is to be appreciative and thankful for the kindness and generosity of other people, as well as for the good fortune and "blessings" of our lives.
- Beneficence. This ideal is defined as performing good acts for their own sake. A popular synonym for beneficence is "random acts of kindness."

Consequences

Consequences are the beneficial or harmful effects—for example, physical, emotional, or financial—that are produced by an action. In many cases, consequences are subtle rather than obvious, complex rather than simple, unintended rather than intended, and delayed rather than immediate. They may also affect many more people than we might at first think. For example, dishonest accounting in a few international corporations could affect investors around the globe and weaken the economies of nations. And the use of nuclear weapons could conceivably harm not only the people exposed to the blast but also generations yet unborn.

A STRATEGY FOR MORAL JUDGMENT

Understanding the criteria for moral judgment provides the basis for making sound ethical judgments. We must also become skilled in applying the criteria to moral issues. The following strategy will help you develop that skill. It will also free you from the unfortunate but common habit of responding to moral issues on the basis of feeling or rash judgment. Whenever you are discussing any issue involving considerations of right and wrong, proceed as follows:

Decide What Obligations Are Present

Consider the kinds of relationships involved in the situation—for example, friendship or business—and decide what obligations, if any, are relevant.

Decide What Moral Ideals Are Relevant

Consider the various moral ideals discussed earlier in the chapter—for example, prudence, justice, or loving kindness—and decide which ones are relevant to the situation you are evaluating. Often, two or more are relevant.

Where Conflicts Exist, Assign Priorities

Determine whether any conflicts exist between obligations, between ideals, or between an obligation and an ideal. For example, if you were discussing the morality of the welfare system in America, you might decide that as representatives of the people, the government has a moral obligation to help citizens who lack adequate food, shelter, and clothing. But you might also decide that the welfare system does recipients an injustice by creating a sense of dependency that robs them and their children of initiative and confidence. In this case, an obligation would be in conflict with a moral ideal (justice). You would then decide, in light of the specific details of the situation, whether the obligation or the ideal deserves higher priority.

Identify Possible Actions and Their Consequences

When people are found to have done something morally wrong, they often say, "What else could I have done?" Equally often, anyone who hears their lament will be able to think of several things they could have done instead, any one of which would have produced better consequences. If you have ever encountered such a situation, you might have wondered, "The other possible actions were so obvious, how could those involved have failed to consider them?" The answer in most cases is that they didn't take the time to identify alternative actions but just acted on the first one that came to mind.

To avoid their mistake, *take the time*. Consider all possible actions and try to identify the probable consequences, beneficial and harmful, of each. Be sure to include not only the consequences to the person taking the action but also the consequences to others as well.

Decide Which Action Is Most Moral

Sometimes this decision will be relatively easy to make; that is, the obligations and ideals will support the same action, and the consequences of that action will all be positive. More often than not, however, two obligations or an obligation and an ideal will be in opposition, or the consequences will be so mixed that none of the choices open to you seems acceptable. Such situations are called moral dilemmas. When you are forced to choose between two actions, each of which is good, choose the one that represents the greater good. When the choice is between two harmful actions, choose the one that represents the lesser harm.

APPLYING THE STRATEGY

To illustrate how helpful this approach can be, let's apply it to two ethical issues. The first occurred some years ago when a mentally unstable man called a television newsroom and threatened to kill himself. The station notified the police and then dispatched a camera crew to the scene. The crew reportedly stood by, filming, while the man doused himself with lighter fluid and lit first one match, then another, in an unsuccessful attempt to ignite himself. The crew moved in to stop him only after he tried a third time and succeeded. The television station subsequently ran the film footage on the air. When some viewers questioned the morality of the camera crew's decision not to intervene sooner, one crew member explained, "My job is to record events as they happen."

The camera crew did have an *obligation* to their employer and, by extension, to the station's viewers to carry out their assignment. But that obligation was in conflict with at least two *moral ideals*—loving kindness and beneficence. The main *consequence* of honoring the obligation rather than the ideals was to endanger the man's life. By honoring the ideals instead of the obligation, the crew could have avoided that risk. Moreover, if one member of the crew had continued to film while the others had prevented the man from igniting himself, the station would have been able to report an act of heroism. In light of these considerations, you would no doubt decide that the camera crew's response was morally deficient.

The second issue concerns the dismissal of a university professor. We'll call him Dr. Woeful and the institution, Benighted University. During the eight years Dr. Woeful had been at B.U., his teaching was, to put it charitably, uninspiring. However, he had published more than the required number of scholarly articles, so was granted tenure. Shortly thereafter, several of his colleagues discovered that most of his publications, including his doctoral dissertation, had been plagiarized. After reviewing the documentation, a faculty committee recommended that Dr. Woeful be dismissed. The administration accepted the recommendation. But Dr. Woeful refused to go quietly, demanding two years' salary, a letter of recommendation from the dean, and a promise that the record of the proceedings against him would be sealed. If B.U. rejected these demands, he said, he would file a discrimination suit against both the university and the colleagues who reported his intellectual dishonesty. The administration reluctantly accepted Dr. Woeful's terms. But was this decision ethical?

The administration had three obligations: to uphold the university's integrity by dismissing Dr. Woeful, to uphold the integrity of the teaching profession by denying Dr. Woeful a recommendation, and to spare the university the financial cost and embarrassment of a lengthy court action. However, the conditions he set made it necessary to choose between the second and third obligations. The administration's decision assigned the financial good of the university a higher priority than the integrity of the teaching profession. Among the consequences of this decision were that Dr. Woeful was, in effect, rewarded for his dishonesty and the students of some other university were more likely to be blighted by his presence. Some would argue that B.U. administration's decision served the greater good and was therefore ethical. Others would disagree.

The strategies discussed in this chapter and the preceding chapters are designed to cultivate the greatest of all natural resources—the human mind. Once you master these strategies and put them to everyday use, you will be on the way to overcoming the deficiencies of your formal education, resisting victimization by specious ideas and irrational impulses, and dealing more effectively with problems and issues. In short, you will be making your mind matter.

APPENDIX

Making Discussion Meaningful

To do all the talking and not be willing to listen is a form of greed.

—Democritus of Abdera

At its best, discussion deepens understanding and illuminates issues. At its worst, it frays nerves, creates animosity, and leaves issues unresolved. Unfortunately, the most prominent models for discussion in contemporary culture—radio and TV talk shows—often produce the latter effects.

Many hosts demand that their guests answer complex questions with simple "yes" or "no" answers. If the guests respond that way, they are attacked for oversimplifying. If, instead, they try to offer a balanced answer, the host shouts, "You're not answering the question" and proceeds to answer it himself or herself. Guests who agree with the host are treated warmly; others are dismissed as ignorant or dishonest. Often as not, when two guests are debating, each takes a turn interrupting while the other shouts, "Let me finish." Neither demonstrates any desire to learn from the other. Typically, as the show draws to a close, the host thanks the participants for a "vigorous debate" and promises (threatens?) more of the same next time.

Here are some simple guidelines for ensuring that the discussions you engage in are more civil, meaningful, and productive than what you see on TV. Follow them even if others do not. In time, they may emulate your good example.

WHENEVER POSSIBLE, PREPARE IN ADVANCE

Not every discussion can be prepared for in advance, but many can—for example, those for which an agenda or schedule is distributed. Use this advance information to prepare for discussion. Begin by reflecting on what you already know about the topic. Then decide how you can expand your knowledge and devote some time to doing so. (Fifteen or twenty minutes of focused searching on the Internet can produce a significant amount of information on almost any subject.) Finally, try to anticipate the different points of view that might be expressed in the discussion and consider the relative merits of each. Keep your conclusions tentative at this point, so that you will be open to the facts and interpretations others will present.

SET REASONABLE EXPECTATIONS

Have you ever left a discussion disappointed that others hadn't abandoned their views and embraced yours? Have you ever felt offended when someone disagreed with you or asked you what evidence you had to support your viewpoint? If the answer to either question is yes, you probably expect too much of others. People seldom change their minds easily or quickly, particularly in the case of long-held convictions. And when they encounter ideas that differ from their own, they naturally want to know what evidence supports those ideas. Expect to have your ideas questioned, and be cheerful and gracious in responding.

LEAVE EGOTISM AND PERSONAL AGENDAS AT THE DOOR

To be productive, discussion requires an atmosphere of mutual respect and civility. Egotism produces disrespectful attitudes toward others—notably, "I'm more important than other people," "My ideas are better than anyone else's," and "Rules don't apply to me." Personal agendas, such as dislike for another participant or excessive zeal for a point of view, can lead to an unwillingness to listen to others' views and, in extreme cases, to verbal attacks on the other person.

CONTRIBUTE BUT DON'T DOMINATE

If you are the kind of person who loves to talk and has a lot to say, you probably contribute more to discussions than other participants do. On the other hand, if you are more reserved, you may seldom say anything. There is nothing wrong with being either kind of person. However, discussions tend to be most productive when everyone contributes ideas. For this to happen, loquacious people need to exercise a little restraint, and more reserved people need to accept responsibility for sharing their thoughts.

AVOID DISTRACTING SPEECH MANNERISMS

Such mannerisms include starting one sentence and then abruptly switching to another, mumbling or slurring your words, and punctuating every phrase or clause with audible pauses ("um," "ah,") or meaningless expressions ("like," "you know," "man"). These annoying mannerisms distract people from your message. To overcome them, listen to yourself when you speak. Even better, tape your conversations with friends and family (with their permission), then play the tape back and determine how you can improve. And whenever you are engaged in a discussion, aim for clarity, directness, and economy of expression.

LISTEN ACTIVELY

When people don't listen to one another, discussion becomes little more than serial monologue, with each person taking a turn at speaking and then ignoring what the others have to say. Listening problems can be traced to the fact that the mind can receive and process ideas faster than the fastest speaker can deliver them. Whenever the mind gets tired of waiting, it wanders about aimlessly like a dog off its leash. You may be familiar with what happens then. Instead of listening to the speaker's words, you think about her clothing or hairstyle, or look outside the window and observe what is happening there. Or perhaps the speaker's words trigger an unrelated memory and you slip away to that earlier time and place. If the speaker says something you disagree with, you begin framing a reply. Be alert for such distractions and make an effort to resist them. Strive to enter the speaker's frame of mind, to understand each sentence as it is spoken, and to connect it with previous sentences. Whenever you realize that your mind is wandering, drag it back to the task.

JUDGE IDEAS RESPONSIBLY

Ideas range in quality from profound to ridiculous, helpful to harmful, ennobling to degrading. It is therefore appropriate to pass judgment on them. However, fairness demands that you base your judgment on thoughtful consideration of the overall strengths and weaknesses of the ideas, not on your initial impressions or feelings. Be especially careful with ideas that are unfamiliar or different from your own because those are the ones you will be most inclined to deny a fair hearing.

RESIST THE URGE TO SHOUT OR INTERRUPT

No doubt you understand that shouting and interrupting are rude and disrespectful behaviors, but do you realize that in many cases they are also signs of intellectual insecurity? It's true. If you really believe your ideas are sound, you will have no need to raise your voice or to silence the other person. Even if the other person resorts to such behavior, the best way to demonstrate confidence and character is by refusing to reciprocate. Make it your rule to disagree without being disagreeable. Keep in mind Stanley Horowitz's insight, "Nothing lowers the level of conversation more than raising the voice."

NOTES

INTRODUCTION

1. For a detailed and interesting discussion of Yerkes and the Hereditarians, see Stephen Jay Gould's *The Mismeasure of Man* (New York: Norton, 1981), chapter 5.

2. Cited in Gould, *The Mismeasure of Man*, 161.

3. Paolo Lionni and Lance J. Klass, *The Leipzig Connection: The Systematic Destruction of American Education* (Portland, Ore.: Heron, 1980), 44.

4. Lionni and Klass, *The Leipzig Connection*, 62.

5. Richard Hofstadter, *Anti-Intellectualism in American Life* (New York: Vintage, 1963), 334–43.

6. Ray Marshall and Marc Tucker, *Thinking for a Living: Education and the Wealth of Nations* (New York: Basic Books, 1992), 80.

7. Harry A. Overstreet, *Mature Mind* (New York: Norton, 1959), 250–51.

8. Irving Babbitt, *Rousseau and Romanticism*, introduction by Claes G. Ryn (New Brunswick, N.J.: Transaction, 1991). Originally published in 1919.

9. Quoted in Hofstadter, *Anti-Intellectualism in American Life*, 87.

10. Mark A. Knoll, *The Scandal of the Evangelical Mind* (Grand Rapids, Mich.: Eerdmans, 1994), 3.

11. Quoted in Knoll, *The Scandal of the Evangelical Mind*, 23.

12. Dewey's *How We Think* (1910, 1933) contains insights that remain valuable today.

13. See Hofstadter, *Anti-Intellectualism in American Life*, 365–70.

14. For a more thorough discussion of Dewey's educational ideas, see Hofstadter, *Anti-Intellectualism in American Life*, especially pages 368–77.

15. Hofstadter, *Anti-Intellectualism in American Life*, 268.

16. Paul C. Vitz, *Psychology as Religion: The Cult of Self-Worship*, 2nd ed. (Grand Rapids, Mich.: Eerdmans, 1994), 99–110.

17. Carl R. Rogers, *On Becoming a Person* (Boston: Houghton-Mifflin, 1961), 22, 194, 23, 27, 189, 289, and 299, respectively.

18. Carl R. Rogers, *A Way of Being* (Boston: Houghton-Mifflin, 1980), 43.

19. Abraham H. Maslow, *Motivation and Personality*, 2nd ed. (New York: Harper & Row, 1970), xix.

20. Richard J. Lowry, ed., *The Journals of A. H. Maslow*, 2 vols. (Monterey, Calif.: Brooks/Cole, 1979), 154–57, 185–86, 951, and 1147, respectively.

21. For an interesting and authoritative study of intuition, see David G. Myers, *Intuition: Its Powers and Perils* (New Haven, Conn.: Yale University Press, 2002).

CHAPTER 1

1. This is the definition I use in *The Art of Thinking* (New York: Longman, 2001), 2.

2. Margaret A. Hagen, *Whores of the Court: The Fraud of Psychiatric Testimony and the Rape of American Justice* (New York: HarperCollins, 1997), 52.

3. See, for example, Elizabeth F. Loftus, *Eyewitness Testimony* (Cambridge, Mass.: Harvard University Press, 1979; with a new preface by the author, 1996).

4. Christopher Cerf and Victor Navasky, *The Experts Speak* (New York: Villard, 1984, 1998).

5. Thomas Szasz, *Insanity: The Idea and Its Consequences* (New York: John Wiley, 1987; with a new preface by the author, Syracuse, N.Y.: Syracuse University Press, 1990), 243–45.

6. See Judith Reisman and Edward M. Eichel, *Kinsey, Sex, and Fraud* (Lafayette, La.: Huntington House, 1986) and Judith A. Reisman, *"Soft Porn" Plays Hardball* (Lafayette, La.: Huntington House, 1991).

7. The WISE approach was separately copyrighted by Vincent Ryan Ruggiero in 2002 and is used with permission.

CHAPTER 2

1. Arnold Toynbee, *Surviving the Future* (New York: Oxford University Press, 1971), quoted in Karl Menninger, *Whatever Became of Sin?* (New York: Hawthorn Books, 1973), 227.

2. Harry Stein, *How I Accidentally Joined the Vast Right-Wing Conspiracy (and Found Inner Peace)* (New York: Delacorte Press, 2000), 64.

3. Columbia Associates in Philosophy, *An Introduction to Reflective Thinking* (Boston: Houghton Mifflin, 1923), 189. See also Paul C. Vitz, *Psychology as Religion: The Cult of Self-Worship*, 2nd ed. (Grand Rapids, Mich.: Eerdmans, 1994), 20.

4. Ned Jones and Richard Nisbett, cited in Robyn M. Dawes, *House of Cards: Psychology and Psychotherapy Built on Myth* (New York: Free Press, 1994), 209.

5. Thomas Gilovich, *How We Know What Isn't So: The Fallibility of Reason in Everyday Life* (New York: Free Press, 1991), 54.

6. Gilovich, *How We Know What Isn't So*, 72.

7. Cited in John Marshall Reeve, *Motivating Others: Nurturing Inner Motivational Resources* (Boston: Allyn & Bacon, 1996), 152.

8. Barbara Lerner, "Self-Esteem and Excellence: The Choice and the Paradox," *American Educator* (winter 1985): 12

9. Dorothy A. Sisk, "What If Your Child Is Gifted?" *American Education* (October 1977).

10. Vitz, *Psychology as Religion*, 10–18.

11. Ken Hamblin, *Plain Talk and Common Sense from the Black Avenger* (New York: Simon & Schuster, 1999), 33–34.

12. Cited in Richard Nisbet and Lee Ross, *Human Inference: Strategies and Shortcomings of Social Judgment* (Englewood Cliffs, N.J.: Prentice-Hall, 1980), 173.

13. Philip Chew Kheng Hoe, ed., *A Gentleman's Code: According to Confucius, Mencius, and Others* (Singapore: Graham Brash, 1984), 36, 47.

14. All these examples are taken from Richard Lederer, *Anguished English* (New York: Dell, 1987).

CHAPTER 3

1. Deborah J. Coon, "'Not a Creature of Reason': The Alleged Impact of Watsonian Behaviorism on Advertising in the 1920s," in *Modern Perspectives on John B. Watson and Classical Behaviorism*, edited by James T. Todd and Edward K. Morris (Westport, Conn.: Greenwood Press, 1994), 37–63.

2. David Cohen, *J. B. Watson: The Founder of Behaviourism* (London: Routledge & Kegan Paul, 1979), 187–88.

3. "Who's Got the Right One," *Consumer Reports* (August 1991): 520.

4. Jerry Mander, *Four Arguments for the Elimination of Television* (New York: Quill, 1978), 303, 310.

5. James Fallows, *Breaking the News* (New York: Pantheon Books, 1996), 118.

6. *Reliable Sources*, CNN, September 20, 1997.

7. Bernard Goldberg, *Bias* (Washington, D.C.: Regnery, 2002), 20.

8. *60 Minutes*, CBS, December 13, 1998.

9. Tammy Bruce, *The New Thought Police* (New York: Prima, 2001), 176–78.

10. Larry Elder, *The Ten Things You Can't Say in America* (New York: St. Martin's, 2000), 107–8.

11. Elder, *Ten Things*, 293–94.

12. *Newswatch*, Fox News Network, March 3, 2001.

13. Robert M. Liebert and Joyce Sprafkin, *The Early Window: Effects of Television on Children and Youth*, 3rd ed. (New York: Pergamon Press, 1988), 149, 153, 155–56.

14. Bruce, *The New Thought Police*, 174.

15. "Confessions of a Tobacco Lobbyist," *60 Minutes*, CBS News, March 19, 1995.

16. Allan Bloom, *The Closing of the American Mind* (New York: Simon & Schuster, 1987), 249.

CHAPTER 4

1. These and many other similar examples may be found in Christopher Cerf and Victor Navasky, *The Experts Speak*, 1st rev. ed. (New York: Villard, 1998).

2. Cited in Michael Medved, *Hollywood vs. America* (New York: HarperCollins, 1992), 241.

3. For the evolution of this changes in viewpoint, see pages 793, 914, 949, 959, and 1115 of *The Journals of A. H. Maslow*, 2 vols., edited by Richard J. Lowry (Monterey, Calif.: Brooks/Cole, 1979).

4. Carol Tavris, *Anger: The Misunderstood Emotion* (New York: Simon & Schuster, 1982), 131–35.

5. Quoted in Tavris, *Anger*, 123.

6. Hannity and Colmes, Fox News Network, April 17, 2001.

CHAPTER 5

1. Margaret A. Hagen, *Whores of the Court: The Fraud of Psychiatric Testimony and the Rape of American Justice* (New York: HarperCollins, 1997), 33, 36.

2. Robert H. Bork, *Slouching towards Gomorrah* (New York: Regan Books, 1996), 144.

3. Christopher Cerf and Victor Navasky, *The Experts Speak*, 1st rev. ed. (New York: Villard, 1998), 6, 332.

4. Hagen, *Whores of the Court*, 285.

5. Marjorie Rosenberg, "The Mindless Self: Freud Triumphant," *First Things* (December 1991), 16–22.

6. Michael Medved, *Hollywood vs. America* (New York: HarperCollins, 1992), 252.

CHAPTER 6

1. Margaret A. Hagen, *Whores of the Court: The Fraud of Psychiatric Testimony and the Rape of American Justice* (New York: HarperCollins, 1997), 39.

CHAPTER 7

1. Joseph Fletcher, *Situation Ethics: The New Morality* (Philadelphia: Westminster Press, 1966), 39, 44.

2. Norman L. Geisler, "The Collapse of Modern Atheism," in *The Intellectuals Speak Out about God,* edited by Roy Abraham Varghese (Dallas: Lewis & Stanley, 1984), 149.

3. Quoted by Edward T. Oakes, "Discovering the American Aristotle," *First Things* (December 3, 1993).

4. Mortimer J. Adler, *Desires Right and Wrong: The Ethics of Enough* (New York: Macmillan, 1991), 33.

5. Quoted in *The Quotable Johnson: A Topical Compilation of His Wit and Moral Wisdom,* edited by Stephen C. Danckert (San Francisco: Ignatius Press, 1992), 39.

6. Matthew McKay and Patrick Fanning, *Self-Esteem* (New York: St. Martin's Press, 1987), 186.

7. Wayne Dyer, *Your Erroneous Zones* (New York: Funk & Wagnalls, 1976), 90–91.

8. Thomas Sowell, "The Saving Grace of Guilt," Commentary Section, *Tampa Tribune* (May 2, 1999), 6.

9. Quoted in Robyn M. Dawes, *House of Cards: Psychology and Psychotherapy Built on Myth* (New York: Free Press, 1994), 235.

10. Errol E. Harris, "Respect for Persons," *Daedalus* (spring 1969): 113.

BIBLIOGRAPHY

Adler, Mortimer J. *Desires Right and Wrong: The Ethics of Enough*. New York: Macmillan Publishing Co., 1991.

Babbitt, Irving. *Rousseau & Romanticism*. Introduction by Claes G. Ryn. New Brunswick, N.J.: Transaction Publishers, 1991. (Originally published in 1919.)

Bloom, Allan. *The Closing of the American Mind*. New York: Simon & Schuster, 1987.

Bork, Robert H. *Slouching Towards Gomorrah*. New York: ReganBooks, 1996.

Bruce, Tammy. *The New Thought Police*. New York: Prima Publishing, 2001.

Cerf, Christopher and Victor Navasky. *The Experts Speak*. New York: Villard, 1984, 1998.

Chew Kheng Hoe, Philip. *A Gentleman's Code: According to Confucius, Mencius and Others*. Singapore: Graham Brash (Pte) Ltd, 1984.

Cohen, David. *J. B. Watson: The Founder of Behaviourism*. London: Routledge & Kegan Paul, 1979.

Columbia Associates in Philosophy. *An Introduction to Reflective Thinking*. Boston: Houghton Mifflin, 1923.

Coon, Deborah J. "'Not a Creature of Reason': The Alleged Impact of Watsonian Behaviorism on Advertising in the 1920s." *Modern Perspectives on John B. Watson and Classical Behaviorism*, James T. Todd & Edward K. Morris, editors. Westport, Conn.: Greenwood Press, 1994.

Danckert, Stephen C., editor. *The Quotable Johnson: A Topical Compilation of His Wit and Moral Wisdom*. San Francisco: Ignatius Press, 1992.

Dawes, Robyn M. *House of Cards: Psychology and Psychotherapy Built on Myth*. New York: The Free Press, 1994.

Dewey, John. *How We Think*. New York: D. C. Heath & Co., 1910, 1933.

Dyer, Wayne. *Your Erroneous Zones*. New York: Funk & Wagnalls, 1976.

Elder, Larry. *The Ten Things You Can't Say in America*. New York: St. Martin's, 2000.

Fallows, James. *Breaking the News*. New York: Pantheon Books. 1996.

Fletcher, Joseph. *Situation Ethics: The New Morality*. Philadelphia: Westminster Press, 1966.

Geisler, Norman L. "The Collapse of Modern Atheism." *The Intellectuals Speak Out About God*, Roy Abraham Varghese, editor. Dallas: Lewis & Stanley, Publishers, 1984.

Gilovich, Thomas, *How We Know What Isn't So: The Fallibility of Reason in Everyday Life*. New York: Free Press, 1991.

Goldberg, Bernard. *Bias*. Washington, D.C.: Regnery Publishing, 2002.

Gould, Stephen Jay. *The Mismeasure of Man*. New York: W. W. Norton & Co., 1981.

Hagen, Margaret A. *Whores of the Court: The Fraud of Psychiatric Testimony and the Rape of American Justice*. New York: HarperCollins, 1997.

Hamblin, Ken. *Plain Talk and Common Sense from the Black Avenger*. New York: Simon & Schuster, 1999.

Harris, Errol E. "Respect for Persons." *Daedalus*, Spring 1969.

Hofstadter, Richard. *Anti-Intellectualism in American Life*. New York: Vintage, 1963.

Knoll, Mark A. *The Scandal of the Evangelical Mind*. Grand Rapids, Mich.: Wm. B. Eerdmans, 1994.

Lerner, Barbara. "Self-Esteem and Excellence: the Choice and the Paradox." *American Educator*, Winter 1985.

Liebert, Robert M. and Joyce Sprafkin. *The Early Window: Effects of Television on Children and Youth*, 3rd edition. New York: Pergamon Press, 1988.

Lionni, Paolo and Lance J. Klass. *The Leipzig Connection: The Systematic Destruction of American Education*. Portland, Oreg.: Heron Books, 1980.

Loftus, Elizabeth F. *Eyewitness Testimony*. Cambridge, Mass.: Harvard University Press, 1979.

Lowry, Richard J., editor. *The Journals of A. H. Maslow*, 2 volumes. Monterey, Calif.: Brooks/Cole Publishing Co., 1979.

Mander, Jerry. *Four Arguments for the Elimination of Television*. New York: Quill, 1978.

Marshall, Ray and Marc Tucker. *Thinking for a Living: Education and the Wealth of Nations*. New York: Basic Books, 1992.

Maslow, Abraham H. *Motivation and Personality*, 2nd edition. New York: Harper & Row, 1970.

McKay, Matthew and Patrick Fanning. *Self-Esteem*. New York: St. Martin's Press, 1987.

Medved, Michael. *Hollywood vs. America*. New York: HarperCollins, 1992.

Menninger, Karl. *Whatever Became of Sin?* New York: Hawthorn Books, Inc., 1973.

Nisbet, Richard and Lee Ross, *Human Inference: Strategies and Shortcomings of Social Judgment*. Englewood Cliffs, N.J.: Prentice-Hall, 1980.

Oakes, Edward T. "Discovering the American Aristotle," *First Things*, December 3, 1993.

Overstreet, Harry A. *The Mature Mind*. New York: Norton, 1949, 1959.

Reeve, John Marshall. *Motivating Others: Nurturing Inner Motivational Resources*. Boston: Allyn & Bacon, 1996.

Reisman, Judith A. *"Soft Porn" Plays Hardball*. Lafayette, La.: Huntington House, 1991.

Reisman, Judith A. and Edward M. Eichel. *Kinsey, Sex, and Fraud*. Lafayette, La.: Huntington House, 1986.

Rogers, Carl R. *On Becoming a Person*. Boston: Houghton-Mifflin, 1961.

———. *A Way of Being*. Boston: Houghton Mifflin Co., 1980.

Rosenberg, Marjorie. "The Mindless Self: Freud Triumphant." *First Things*, December 1991.

Sisk, Dorothy A. "What If Your Child Is Gifted?" *American Education*, October 1977.

Sowell, Thomas. "The Saving Grace of Guilt," Commentary Section, *Tampa Tribune*, May 2, 1999.

Stein, Harry. *How I Accidentally Joined the Vast Right-Wing Conspiracy (and Found Inner Peace)*. New York: Delacorte Press, 2000.

Szasz, Thomas. *Insanity: The Idea and Its Consequences*. John Wiley & Sons, 1987, 1990.

Tavris, Carol. *Anger: The Misunderstood Emotion*. New York: Simon & Schuster, 1982.

Vitz, Paul C. *Psychology as Religion: The Cult of Self-Worship*. Grand Rapids, Mich.: William. B. Eerdmans, 1977, 1994.

"Who's Got the Right One?" *Consumer Reports*, August 1991.

INDEX

Note: (n) denotes a note number

ABOUT THE AUTHOR

Vincent Ryan Ruggiero, Professor Emeritus, State University of New York at Delhi, has been a social caseworker, an industrial engineer, and a humanities professor. The author of twenty books, he is best known for his pioneering work in the teaching of thinking.

The Elements of Rhetoric (1971) restored the classical emphases on reasoning and persuasion to contemporary rhetoric. *Thinking Critically About Ethical Issues* is a guide to ethical reasoning. *Beyond Feelings* offers a strategy for disciplined, logical thought. *The Art of Thinking* combines creative thinking and critical thinking into a single heuristic for solving problems and making decisions. *Teaching Thinking Across the Curriculum* demonstrates how to integrate thinking instruction with traditional subject matter.

Other books by Professor Ruggiero include *The Art of Writing, Good Habits, Warning: Nonsense Is Destroying America*, and *Changing Attitudes*.

Professor Ruggiero enjoys an international reputation as a speaker and seminar leader on the role of thinking in educational and social reform. He may be contacted through his website: www.mindpower-inc.com.